100
DAYS
in the
NEW
TESTAMENT

B&H
PUBLISHING GROUP

NASHVILLE, TENNESSEE

978-1-4336-4918-9

Published by B&H Publishing Group
Nashville, Tennessee

Custom edition published for LifeWay Christian Stores.

1 2 3 4 5 6 7 • 20 19 18 17 16

Contents

Introduction

The Bible takes history and divides it in half; the time before Jesus came to Earth, and the time after His resurrection. Just like we are today, the people in the New Testament were living in the after. The early church had all the same questions we still have today and had the same desire to grow closer to God.

If you have spent any time reading the Bible, you've most likely had at least some experience and exposure to all of the stories you are about to read; but this is a chance to focus in and meditate on the individual details Scripture gives us about the early church, and the questions and problems they faced. This devotional is meant to be a magnifying glass to help you focus in and sit in passages from the New Testament that we too often skim over and lose the full impact.

Whether you choose to read them one a day, one a week, or at whatever speed you choose, you'll be keeping the Word in the center of your thoughts and growing in your walk with Christ.

Matthew 28:1–10
The Greatest News

After the Sabbath, as the first day of the week was dawning, Mary Magdalene and the other Mary went to view the tomb. Suddenly there was a violent earthquake, because an angel of the Lord descended from heaven and approached the tomb. He rolled back the stone and was sitting on it. His appearance was like lightning, and his robe was as white as snow. The guards were so shaken from fear of him that they became like dead men.

But the angel told the women, "Don't be afraid, because I know you are looking for Jesus who was crucified. He is not here! For He has been resurrected, just as He said. Come and see the place where He lay. Then go quickly and tell His disciples, 'He has been raised from the dead. In fact, He is going ahead of you to Galilee; you will see Him there.' Listen, I have told you."

So, departing quickly from the tomb with fear and great joy, they ran to tell His disciples the news. Just then Jesus met them and said, "Good morning!" They came up, took hold of His feet, and worshiped Him. Then Jesus told them, "Do not be afraid. Go and tell My brothers to leave for Galilee, and they will see Me there."

When something wonderful happens to you—the birth of a baby, a relationship restored, a job promotion, even a great sale at your favorite store—what is the first thing you want to do? You want to tell someone! Your need to tell others is often even more profound if the wonderful thing was preceded by something terrible, like what happened in today's passage with the women at the tomb.

Mary Magdalene and Mary were deep in despair when they arrived at Jesus' tomb on the first day of the week. They had seen Jesus die on the cross and were present when His body was laid in the tomb. It had seemed as if all was lost.

As was their burial custom, the women went to anoint Jesus' body with oil and spices (see Mark 16:1). They had no idea what they were about to experience.

The Scripture says an angel came down, rolled away the stone from the tomb's opening, and spoke to them. The angel told them not to be afraid, but to run and tell the disciples that Jesus was alive and would see them in Galilee! Can you imagine the joy?

Do you think the angel really had to tell them to share that news? Don't you imagine they could not possibly have been silent when they had the greatest news of all time?

We have also heard this greatest news of all time. An angel hasn't appeared to us to entreat us to tell others the news, but how can we be silent? Jesus has risen! He is alive!

Galatians 2:11–21
Whose Life Are You Living?

But when Cephas came to Antioch, I opposed him to his face because he stood condemned. For he regularly ate with the Gentiles before certain men came from James. However, when they came, he withdrew and separated himself, because he feared those from the circumcision party. Then the rest of the Jews joined his hypocrisy, so that even Barnabas was carried away by their hypocrisy. But when I saw that they were deviating from the truth of the gospel, I told Cephas in front of everyone, "If you, who are a Jew, live like a Gentile and not like a Jew, how can you compel Gentiles to live like Jews?"

We who are Jews by birth and not "Gentile sinners" know that no one is justified by the works of the law but by faith in Jesus Christ. And we have believed in Christ Jesus so that we might be justified by faith in Christ and not by the works of the law, because by the works of the law no human being will be justified. But if we ourselves are also found to be "sinners" while seeking to be justified by Christ, is Christ then a promoter of sin? Absolutely not! If I rebuild the system I tore down, I show myself to be a lawbreaker. For through the law I have died to the law, so that I might live for God. I have been crucified with Christ and I no longer live, but Christ

lives in me. The life I now live in the body, I live by
faith in the Son of God, who loved me and gave
Himself for me. I do not set aside the grace of
God, for if righteousness comes through the law,
then Christ died for nothing.

A prince in rags. A poor boy as surrogate king. Mark Twain's grip-
ping tale of mistaken identity, *The Prince and the Pauper,* has
intrigued readers since it was first published in 1882. One boy roamed
the streets despite being destined for the throne, while the other was
pampered in royalty, though he was born to poverty—all as the result
of merely exchanging garments.

Like a pauper-made-king, we can be tempted to overvalue our
exchanged identity in Christ by boasting in who we have become.
Although our inadequacies are evident, we spend our lives trying to
prove otherwise. Like Cephas, Barnabas, and the other Jews mentioned
in the passage above, we often strive harder in our standing before others than with our kneeling before God.

Yet, our life is not ours now to live. Our insides are not merely a
cleaned-up version of our old selves, but literally Christ's very breath
within us. "Christ lives in me." The focus isn't upon our pampered
royalty, but upon Him as our energizing Source.

Mark 1:35–44

Champion of Compassion

Very early in the morning, while it was still dark, He got up, went out, and made His way to a deserted place. And He was praying there. Simon and his companions went searching for Him. They found Him and said, "Everyone's looking for You!"

And He said to them, "Let's go on to the neighboring villages so that I may preach there too. This is why I have come." So He went into all of Galilee, preaching in their synagogues and driving out demons.

Then a man with a serious skin disease came to Him and, on his knees, begged Him: "If You are willing, You can make me clean."

Moved with compassion, Jesus reached out His hand and touched him. "I am willing," He told him. "Be made clean." Immediately the disease left him, and he was healed. Then He sternly warned him and sent him away at once, telling him, "See that you say nothing to anyone; but go and show yourself to the priest, and offer what Moses prescribed for your cleansing, as a testimony to them."

What is considered the worst disease today? HIV/AIDS? Lupus? Diabetes? Cancer? Ebola? Alzheimer's? Perhaps it depends on which one ravages you or your loved one. Regardless of the disease, there is one thing we all want—for the person with the ailment to be healed.

In the Old and New Testaments, it seemed to be the general consensus that leprosy was the worst disease. It was chronic, it was infectious, and it made the person ceremonially unclean. In some instances, it caused others to think the person with it had committed an unforgivable sin. Leprosy made people untouchable, as outcasts in society—that is, until Jesus came around.

Jesus was a man of compassion. He was never overwhelmed with the sick, the hurting, the possessed, or the outcast. He was simply full of compassion toward them. Jesus was a great example and promoter of compassion as He stopped to heal the ones His Father asked Him to heal.

In this verse, Jesus was not only able to heal the man with leprosy; He was "willing" (v. 41). We never read in Scripture of a time when Jesus was unwilling to heal someone. In fact, He often did more than heal them physically; He also healed them spiritually. He would forgive them of their sins, and He would restore their bodies.

As Jesus overtakes our hearts, how willing should we be to run to those who are hurting? Are we willing to do what is asked of us in order to be healed, as well as to lead others to Jesus so He can heal their bodies and save their souls?

Romans 1:1–15
The Gospel

Paul, a slave of Christ Jesus, called as an apostle and singled out for God's good news—which He promised long ago through His prophets in the Holy Scriptures—concerning His Son, Jesus Christ our Lord, who was a descendant of David according to the flesh and who has been declared to be the powerful Son of God by the resurrection from the dead according to the Spirit of holiness. We have received grace and apostleship through Him to bring about the obedience of faith among all the nations, on behalf of His name, including yourselves who also belong to Jesus Christ by calling:

To all who are in Rome, loved by God, called as saints.

Grace to you and peace from God our Father and the Lord Jesus Christ.

First, I thank my God through Jesus Christ for all of you because the news of your faith is being reported in all the world. For God, whom I serve with my spirit in telling the good news about His Son, is my witness that I constantly mention you, always asking in my prayers that if it is somehow in God's will, I may now at last succeed in coming to you. For I want very much to see you, so I may impart to you some spiritual gift to strengthen you, that is, to be mutually encouraged by each other's faith, both yours and mine.

Now I want you to know, brothers, that I often planned to come to you (but was prevented until now) in order that I might have a fruitful ministry among you, just as among the rest of the Gentiles. I am obligated both to Greeks and barbarians, both to the wise and the foolish. So I am eager to preach the good news to you also who are in Rome.

In introducing himself to the church in Rome, Paul began with one sentence, one thought that runs for seven verses in our Bibles. He told the believers, living in the heart of the most powerful empire in the world at that time, the "Who" of the gospel.

The gospel cannot be separated from Jesus. He is the gospel message.

Paul reminded the church that the gospel is more powerful than death. Jesus was "declared" the Son of God with power through the resurrection. The word declared here means He was "marked out with unmistakable signs." Death was brought about by our sin, but in overcoming death, Jesus forever, unmistakably declared Himself to be the Son of God, the Savior of the world. Furthermore, Paul pointed out that this gospel message was not just for the Jews, but also for the Gentiles (both of which comprised the church in Rome).

The message of the gospel is as powerful today as it has ever been. People are still raised to new life by it every day. Our job is simply to declare that powerful message today to all people. Ask God to help you be bold in declaring the power of the gospel.

Colossians 3:1–15
Heavenly Focus

So if you have been raised with the Messiah, seek what is above, where the Messiah is, seated at the right hand of God. Set your minds on what is above, not on what is on the earth. For you have died, and your life is hidden with the Messiah in God. When the Messiah, who is your life, is revealed, then you also will be revealed with Him in glory.

Therefore, put to death what belongs to your worldly nature: sexual immorality, impurity, lust, evil desire, and greed, which is idolatry. Because of these, God's wrath comes on the disobedient, and you once walked in these things when you were living in them. But now you must also put away all the following: anger, wrath, malice, slander, and filthy language from your mouth. Do not lie to one another, since you have put off the old self with its practices and have put on the new self. You are being renewed in knowledge according to the image of your Creator. In Christ there is not Greek and Jew, circumcision and uncircumcision, barbarian, Scythian, slave and free; but Christ is all and in all.

Therefore, God's chosen ones, holy and loved, put on heartfelt compassion, kindness, humility, gentleness, and patience, accepting one another

*and forgiving one another if anyone has a com-
plaint against another. Just as the Lord has forgiven
you, so you must also forgive. Above all, put on
love—the perfect bond of unity. And let the peace
of the Messiah, to which you were also called in
one body, control your hearts. Be thankful.*

Paul, writing from prison, exhorts the believers in Colossae to live with their hearts and minds focused on heaven. This is not our natural inclination. Our natural drift is toward the things of this world.

In his *Colossians and Philemon MacArthur New Testament Commentary,* Volume 12, John MacArthur wrote: "The believer's whole disposition should orient itself toward heaven, where Christ is, just as a compass needle orients itself toward the north." Christ is our true north.

It takes intentional effort to turn our minds and hearts toward heaven. We are more likely to think about our next project, our next relationship, or our next big thing than we are to think about heaven. Not that we shouldn't concentrate on the here and now. We just have to keep it in the right perspective, making minor (or major) adjustments in our lives to stay centered on our true north.

Since we have been raised with Christ, we are no longer to be distracted and pulled away by the things of this world. We have a new life with Christ. Once we were raised with Christ, we became intimately bound with Him. The next time you feel the world dragging you down and are disoriented, look up!

Quote: John MacArthur, *MacArthur New Testament Commentary,* vol. 12 (Chicago, IL: Moody Publishers, 1992).

1 Corinthians 6:12–20
Prized Possessions

"Everything is permissible for me," but not everything is helpful. "Everything is permissible for me," but I will not be brought under the control of anything. "Food for the stomach and the stomach for food," but God will do away with both of them. The body is not for sexual immorality but for the Lord, and the Lord for the body. God raised up the Lord and will also raise us up by His power. Don't you know that your bodies are a part of Christ's body? So should I take a part of Christ's body and make it part of a prostitute? Absolutely not! Don't you know that anyone joined to a prostitute is one body with her? For Scripture says, The two will become one flesh. But anyone joined to the Lord is one spirit with Him.

Run from sexual immorality! "Every sin a person can commit is outside the body." On the contrary, the person who is sexually immoral sins against his own body. Don't you know that your body is a sanctuary of the Holy Spirit who is in you, whom you have from God? You are not your own, for you were bought at a price. Therefore glorify God in your body.

Consider the special objects in your home. What are the mementos you've kept or the heirlooms that have been passed down to you? What are your prized possessions?

You are the prized possession of God. He deeply desires to keep you from self-inflicted harm. Paul taught believers to flee from any type of immorality and specifically teaches here against such sin. Interestingly, Paul preaches against the immorality from the position that it is a sin against our own body. The Bible is clear that all sin is primarily against God but now we can gain another layer of understanding. Sin profanes our own bodies.

The presence of the Holy Spirit makes our bodies God's dwelling place, His holy sanctuary. Part of what this means is that God's presence in us calls for us to treat our bodies with respect. His presence makes our bodies holy, so that we must avoid anything that would degrade them. Rather, we are to treat them with dignity and care so they will honor God.

Another part of what this means is that because God's Spirit dwells in us continually, we can worship Him in spirit and truth at any time. He never leaves us. He is always there. Our fellowship with Him is continual—now and for eternity.

As a Christian, we do not go to a building that is a temple housing the presence of God. We are temples that the Holy Spirit inhabits. Our actions should reflect that truth. We are to protect ourselves in order to retain our witness of God's glory.

Luke 11:1–13
The Model Prayer

He was praying in a certain place, and when He finished, one of His disciples said to Him, "Lord, teach us to pray, just as John also taught his disciples."

He said to them, "Whenever you pray, say:

Father, Your name be honored as holy. Your kingdom come. Give us each day our daily bread. And forgive us our sins, for we ourselves also forgive everyone in debt to us. And do not bring us into temptation."

He also said to them: "Suppose one of you has a friend and goes to him at midnight and says to him, 'Friend, lend me three loaves of bread, because a friend of mine on a journey has come to me, and I don't have anything to offer him.' Then he will answer from inside and say, 'Don't bother me! The door is already locked, and my children and I have gone to bed. I can't get up to give you anything.' I tell you, even though he won't get up and give him anything because he is his friend, yet because of his friend's persistence, he will get up and give him as much as he needs.

"So I say to you, keep asking, and it will be given to you. Keep searching, and you will find. Keep knocking, and the door will be opened to you. For everyone who asks receives, and the one

who searches finds, and to the one who knocks,
the door will be opened. What father among you, if
his son asks for a fish, will give him a snake instead
of a fish? Or if he asks for an egg, will give him a
scorpion? If you then, who are evil, know how to
give good gifts to your children, how much more
will the heavenly Father give the Holy Spirit to those
who ask Him?"

Many of us have prayed the Lord's Prayer in a corporate setting since we were children. We know the King-James Matthew 6 version by heart. But when we pray it, how often do we pay attention to what we're saying? Are we actually praying, or are we simply reciting it?

When we really look at and think about this prayer, we see several aspects emerge: adoration ("Your name be honored as holy"), petition ("Give us each day our daily bread"), and confession ("Forgive us our sins"). Jesus simply modeled the basic parts of prayer for us.

Did He intend for us to simply pray this one prayer over and over? It's unlikely. After all, He said it in response to a disciple asking Him to teach them how to pray. And it's recorded a little differently here in Luke than it was in Matthew. It's assumed that He was teaching His disciples how to pray more than the exact what to pray.

And He also tells us that when we pray, God will hear us. We are to persist in prayer, and He will respond. Like an earthly father gives his children good gifts, our heavenly Father will give us what we need when we need it.

Right now, take some time to pray as Jesus did, not with His exact words, but with the intention laid out in His model prayer.

Acts 1:1–11
You Will Be My Witnesses

I wrote the first narrative, Theophilus, about all that Jesus began to do and teach until the day He was taken up, after He had given orders through the Holy Spirit to the apostles He had chosen. After He had suffered, He also presented Himself alive to them by many convincing proofs, appearing to them during 40 days and speaking about the kingdom of God.

While He was together with them, He commanded them not to leave Jerusalem, but to wait for the Father's promise. "This," He said, "is what you heard from Me; for John baptized with water, but you will be baptized with the Holy Spirit not many days from now."

So when they had come together, they asked Him, "Lord, are You restoring the kingdom to Israel at this time?"

He said to them, "It is not for you to know times or periods that the Father has set by His own authority. But you will receive power when the Holy Spirit has come on you, and you will be My witnesses in Jerusalem, in all Judea and Samaria, and to the ends of the earth."

After He had said this, He was taken up as they were watching, and a cloud took Him out of

their sight. While He was going, they were gaz-
ing into heaven, and suddenly two men in white
clothes stood by them. They said, "Men of Galilee,
why do you stand looking up into heaven? This
Jesus, who has been taken from you into heaven,
will come in the same way that you have seen Him
going into heaven."

You will be My witnesses," Jesus said. When we think about "witnessing" to people, we often imagine blatantly sharing the gospel with words. What we often fail to consider, however, is how we witness to others with our other words and with our actions.

Who hinders unbelievers more from coming to Christ—a believer who verbally shares the gospel but whose lifestyle fails to support his words, or a believer who lives a godly life but never speaks about Christ? The hypocrisy of one repels listeners from Jesus while the good deeds of another point only to his or her own goodness, but not to the Savior.

Jesus was going away, but His work would continue because His followers would be His witnesses. Today, Jesus' command to witness is equally as compelling for us as it was for the apostles. Wherever we go, with whomever we encounter, Jesus is counting on us to speak and to live out His message. That's His plan for sharing the gospel throughout the earth.

What about you? Are you faithfully witnessing both in word and deed? Do those you encounter even know you're a Christian? What exactly does your witness tell them about the Savior?

Hebrews 11:8–16
Temporary Residents

By faith Abraham, when he was called, obeyed and went out to a place he was going to receive as an inheritance. He went out, not knowing where he was going. By faith he stayed as a foreigner in the land of promise, living in tents with Isaac and Jacob, coheirs of the same promise. For he was looking forward to the city that has foundations, whose architect and builder is God.

By faith even Sarah herself, when she was unable to have children, received power to conceive offspring, even though she was past the age, since she considered that the One who had promised was faithful. Therefore from one man—in fact, from one as good as dead—came offspring as numerous as the stars of heaven and as innumerable as the grains of sand by the seashore.

These all died in faith without having received the promises, but they saw them from a distance, greeted them, and confessed that they were foreigners and temporary residents on the earth. Now those who say such things make it clear that they are seeking a homeland. If they were thinking about where they came from, they would have had an opportunity to return. But they now desire a better place—a heavenly one. Therefore God is not ashamed to be called their God, for He has prepared a city for them.

When missionaries go out into foreign lands, no matter how many decades they may spend there, they will always be foreigners in that land. They are temporary residents, even though they become part of the people, culture, and language. At the same time, when they go back "home," they often feel like they're not really home there either. There's typically a feeling that they don't fully belong to any one place.

Hebrews 11 provides examples of people who faithfully followed God to faraway places. For example, God called Abraham to leave his native land to go to a place he did not know. God promised him land and offspring too numerous to count. By faith, he went. In Canaan, he lived as a nomad, never possessing the land and never seeing the fulfillment of the promise of numerous offspring. Yet he believed God and His promises. He remained a temporary resident, a foreigner in a strange land. He was a pilgrim or sojourner moving toward God's promises.

The Christian life is like that. We are temporary residents of this world, anticipating the future home God has promised to us. If we feel like we don't fully belong here, it's because we don't! Our true home is in heaven with the Lord, and it will be far better than any home we could have on Earth and, in fact, far more glorious than we can even imagine. So for now, we live by faith and with hope of what is to come.

Acts 2:41-47
The Family of God

*So those who accepted his message were bap-
tized, and that day about 3,000 people were
added to them. And they devoted themselves to
the apostles' teaching, to the fellowship, to the
breaking of bread, and to the prayers.*

*Then fear came over everyone, and many won-
ders and signs were being performed through the
apostles. Now all the believers were together and
held all things in common. They sold their possessions and property and distributed the proceeds to
all, as anyone had a need. Every day they devoted
themselves to meeting together in the temple complex, and broke bread from house to house. They
ate their food with a joyful and humble attitude,
praising God and having favor with all the people.
And every day the Lord added to them those who
were being saved.*

Even in the midst of busy lives, at least twice a year, without missing a beat, most families come together on Thanksgiving and
Christmas. The believers in Acts did a much better job of being a family. They were not satisfied with coming together on special occasions,
or even once a week.

Not long after Jesus ascended into the clouds, what appeared
like tongues of fire descended and settled on the believers who met

together, and they began to speak in other languages (Acts 2:3–4). After Peter stood up to explain what was happening, about three thousand people were baptized and added to the church that day (v. 41). A "family" was formed. They worshipped together, shared in the Lord's Supper, and met together daily. They shared meals in various houses. If someone had a need, others filled it. They truly lived like a family.

How does that compare to how Christians live today? Often, we meet as a huge group once or twice a week for an hour or two in a building that may well be a thirty-minute drive from our homes. And then some of us also meet in smaller groups once a week in someone's home or at a coffee shop. We might "serve the city" together two Saturdays a year.

Why did the early church spend so much time together? We don't know for sure, but there could be several reasons. Perhaps they saw it as the way God would want His children to interact with each other. Maybe there was such persecution from non-believers that they needed to stick together for support. It could have been a cultural thing. Whatever the reason, the Lord impressed Luke to record their family-like actions in his book, so we know it's important.

Does that mean we need to eat every meal with other believers? Should we meet together every day? Maybe, but getting legalistic about it isn't the answer. The point is that those early followers of Jesus lived like the family they were—as sons and daughters of the one true God. We would do well to consider their lifestyle and see if we need to make any changes to ours in order to treat other believers as what they are— our brothers and sisters in Christ.

Matthew 10:37–42
It's Not About Us

The person who loves father or mother more than Me is not worthy of Me; the person who loves son or daughter more than Me is not worthy of Me. And whoever doesn't take up his cross and follow Me is not worthy of Me. Anyone finding his life will lose it, and anyone losing his life because of Me will find it.

"The one who welcomes you welcomes Me, and the one who welcomes Me welcomes Him who sent Me. Anyone who welcomes a prophet because he is a prophet will receive a prophet's reward. And anyone who welcomes a righteous person because he's righteous will receive a righteous person's reward. And whoever gives just a cup of cold water to one of these little ones because he is a disciple—I assure you: He will never lose his reward!"

Many are the stories of those who think they've "arrived" only to find they never really left. People make decisions about what will make them happy; then they pursue it. Often they leave one thing they thought was what life was all about, only to chase after another. Rare is the person who decides early on that, "It's not about me." The one who decides to commit his or her life to Christ and look for God's purpose in life will most certainly find it.

One such person was Nate Saint. Nate took his family to South America to reach the Waodani tribe, and he sadly died before getting to see much accomplished. Members of the murderous, ancient tribe speared him and four other men to death without ever hearing the gospel. The men gave their lives in service to their Lord before they were able to accomplish their goals of telling this unreached people group about the love of Christ.

But Nate's goals were nonetheless fulfilled, because his goals weren't his own; they were God's. His life wasn't his, as he had written a blank check long before. Years later, Nate's son Steve went to the Waodani village and came face-to-face with his father's killer. With a spear in hand, just inches from the other man's heart, Steve forgave the man, stepping back and saying, "Nobody killed my father. My father chose to give his life." This tribesman later gave his heart to Christ. God took bad and brought good, but whether Nate Saint had lived or died, he had shown that he had lost his life for Christ long ago, and therefore, he found it.

We might not be asked to attempt to share the gospel with a hostile people group and literally risk losing our lives, but we must be willing to figuratively lose our lives when God calls us to do so. Are you willing to do so? If not, search your heart and ask God to bring you to a place where you are willing to risk all for Him.

Acts 3:11−20
Leave the Baggage Behind

While he was holding on to Peter and John, all the people, greatly amazed, ran toward them in what is called Solomon's Colonnade. When Peter saw this, he addressed the people: "Men of Israel, why are you amazed at this? Or why do you stare at us, as though we had made him walk by our own power or godliness? The God of Abraham, Isaac, and Jacob, the God of our fathers, has glorified His Servant Jesus, whom you handed over and denied in the presence of Pilate, when he had decided to release Him. But you denied the Holy and Righteous One and asked to have a murderer given to you. You killed the source of life, whom God raised from the dead; we are witnesses of this. By faith in His name, His name has made this man strong, whom you see and know. So the faith that comes through Him has given him this perfect health in front of all of you.

"And now, brothers, I know that you did it in ignorance, just as your leaders also did. But what God predicted through the mouth of all the prophets—that His Messiah would suffer—He has fulfilled in this way. Therefore repent and turn back, so that your sins may be wiped out, that seasons of refreshing may come from the presence of the

Lord, and that He may send Jesus, who has been appointed for you as the Messiah.

One of the hardest things about traveling is keeping up with your luggage. Hauling a suitcase or two through a bustling airport is tiring. Putting it into the overhead bin can be a struggle. And finding a spot for a full-size suitcase on a crowded train can be near to impossible. Baggage can be such a heavy load. Wouldn't travel be so much easier if you didn't have to be burdened with baggage?

Life could also be so much easier if we weren't loaded down with the baggage from our past. Sometimes it seems as if all of the times we messed up, hurt people, and made bad decisions follow us everywhere. We can't get rid of them, and they affect how we live today.

But Peter reminds us in Acts 3 that we don't have to go through life weighed down by the sins of the past. Our sins can be removed so we no longer have to be under the heavy load of guilt and shame. Jesus' sacrifice on the cross gives us strength to press on. As we travel through life, His strength becomes our strength as we place our faith in Him.

If one of the most tiring things about traveling is our baggage, we don't have to carry the baggage alone. The Bible promises us times of refreshing, which will come from the presence of the very Lord of the universe. Set down your baggage, and rest in Him.

Romans 2:12–24
Walk the Walk

*All those who sinned without the law will also per-
ish without the law, and all those who sinned under
the law will be judged by the law. For the hearers
of the law are not righteous before God, but the
doers of the law will be declared righteous. So,
when Gentiles, who do not have the law, instinc-
tively do what the law demands, they are a law
to themselves even though they do not have the
law. They show that the work of the law is written
on their hearts. Their consciences confirm this. Their
competing thoughts will either accuse or excuse
them on the day when God judges what people
have kept secret, according to my gospel through
Christ Jesus.*

*Now if you call yourself a Jew, and rest in the
law, boast in God, know His will, and approve
the things that are superior, being instructed from
the law, and if you are convinced that you are a
guide for the blind, a light to those in darkness, an
instructor of the ignorant, a teacher of the imma-
ture, having the full expression of knowledge and
truth in the law—you then, who teach another, don't
you teach yourself? You who preach, "You must not
steal"—do you steal? You who say, "You must not
commit adultery"—do you commit adultery? You
who detest idols, do you rob their temples? You*

who boast in the law, do you dishonor God by
breaking the law? For, as it is written: The name of
God is blasphemed among the Gentiles because of
you.

We have all had those conversations with unchurched friends or relatives—they tell us that the reason they do not attend church is because of all the hypocrites. Most of us are unsure how to respond, because we know that there are hypocrites in every church. We even may be tempted to judge the hypocrites among us.

This passage reminds us that we should be looking first at our own hearts. Do we live what we say we believe? None of us are perfect; we are all hypocrites in some way and do things that we know and publicly proclaim are wrong. The key is in the way we respond. Do we just go on sinning, pretending as if we're not doing what we know to be wrong? Or do we repent, ask forgiveness from others when it is called for, and acknowledge the role God's grace plays in that incident? That's the difference between a true hypocrite and a sinner who understands the gospel.

This issue of hypocrisy is not a light one. In verse 24, we read, "The name of God is blasphemed among the Gentiles because of you." Hypocrites blaspheme the Lord. That is a serious matter. But when we acknowledge our sins and fall upon God's grace, we show others what the gospel is all about.

2 Peter 1:1–11
Partakers of Divine Nature

Simeon Peter, a slave and an apostle of Jesus Christ:

To those who have obtained a faith of equal privilege with ours through the righteousness of our God and Savior Jesus Christ.

May grace and peace be multiplied to you through the knowledge of God and of Jesus our Lord.

His divine power has given us everything required for life and godliness through the knowledge of Him who called us by His own glory and goodness. By these He has given us very great and precious promises, so that through them you may share in the divine nature, escaping the corruption that is in the world because of evil desires. For this very reason, make every effort to supplement your faith with goodness, goodness with knowledge, knowledge with self-control, self-control with endurance, endurance with godliness, godliness with brotherly affection, and brotherly affection with love. For if these qualities are yours and are increasing, they will keep you from being useless or unfruitful in the knowledge of our Lord Jesus Christ. The person who lacks these things is blind and shortsighted and has forgotten the cleansing from his past sins.

> *Therefore, brothers, make every effort to confirm*
> *your calling and election, because if you do these*
> *things you will never stumble. For in this way, entry*
> *into the eternal kingdom of our Lord and Savior*
> *Jesus Christ will be richly supplied to you.*

We shall be like Jesus. That's the promise of Scripture. The exciting part is the process gets underway the moment we receive Him as Lord and Savior. The process of transformation, the metamorphosis that Scripture calls "sanctification," is lifelong and continuous for believers.

Children often act like their parents. They react to things in similar ways. They tend to follow their parents' lead in areas such as forgiveness, generosity, and self-control. In the same way, God plans for His children to act like Jesus. We are daily being transformed into His image (see 2 Cor. 3:18). As a believer, I should act more like Jesus today than I did yesterday. And tomorrow, even more.

Have you ever noticed that husbands and wives who live together over many years end up looking alike? Studies have shown this to be true. It's due to the fact that they act alike—they eat the same foods, they experience similar amounts of stress, they live in the same climate, they mimic each others' facial expressions, and each typically gets a comparable amount of physical exercise as the other. Basically, they look alike because they have lived alike for decades.

Those who live with Jesus over long lifetimes look more like Him. Their character, their spirit, their strengths, their intimacy with the Father—all attest to the presence of Christ. The more time they spend with Him, the more they mimic His actions and internalize His characteristics.

Titus 2:1–14
Christian Conduct

But you must say the things that are consistent with sound teaching. Older men are to be level headed, worthy of respect, sensible, and sound in faith, love, and endurance. In the same way, older women are to be reverent in behavior, not slanderers, not addicted to much wine. They are to teach what is good, so they may encourage the young women to love their husbands and to love their children, to be self-controlled, pure, homemakers, kind, and submissive to their husbands, so that God's message will not be slandered.

In the same way, encourage the young men to be self-controlled in everything. Make yourself an example of good works with integrity and dignity in your teaching. Your message is to be sound beyond reproach, so that the opponent will be ashamed, having nothing bad to say about us.

Slaves are to be submissive to their masters in everything, and to be well-pleasing, not talking back or stealing, but demonstrating utter faithfulness, so that they may adorn the teaching of God our Savior in everything.

For the grace of God has appeared with salvation for all people, instructing us to deny godlessness and worldly lusts and to live in a sensible,

righteous, and godly way in the present age, while
we wait for the blessed hope and appearing of the
glory of our great God and Savior, Jesus Christ. He
gave Himself for us to redeem us from all lawless-
ness and to cleanse for Himself a people for His
own possession, eager to do good works.

Do you make New Year's resolutions? Losing weight, exercising, eating healthy, reading more, being kinder, or stressing less? What's typically on your list? Whatever it is, it undoubtedly takes discipline to achieve, or you wouldn't need to make a special resolution in order to get it done.

The Bible gives practical advice about how to conduct our lives in ways that are pleasing to God. Sometimes this advice does not come easily. It requires discipline, just like those resolutions do.

When Paul wrote to Titus, a Gentile follower of Christ who was leading the church in Crete, some members of the church were struggling with proper Christian behavior. Paul challenged these believers not to give in to ungodliness and worldly lusts. Ungodliness can describe any behavior that is disobedient to God's way. Lust describes not only sexual sins, but giving in to any kind of sinful desires. Instead of giving in, we are to pursue sober living, righteousness, and godliness.

Yes, these are the qualities God desires for those who follow Him. The tricky part is we have to do this in the broken, sin-filled world we call home. But we are not alone in our endeavors. We have Christian brothers and sisters to help us and keep us accountable, and we have God Himself, in the form of the Holy Spirit, living inside us. There can be no greater help than that!

Hebrews 5:1–10
The Author of Salvation

For every high priest taken from men is appointed in service to God for the people, to offer both gifts and sacrifices for sins. He is able to deal gently with those who are ignorant and are going astray, since he is also subject to weakness. Because of this, he must make a sin offering for himself as well as for the people. No one takes this honor on himself; instead, a person is called by God, just as Aaron was. In the same way, the Messiah did not exalt Himself to become a high priest, but the One who said to Him, You are My Son; today I have become Your Father, also said in another passage, You are a priest forever in the order of Melchizedek.

During His earthly life, He offered prayers and appeals with loud cries and tears to the One who was able to save Him from death, and He was heard because of His reverence. Though He was God's Son, He learned obedience through what He suffered. After He was perfected, He became the source of eternal salvation for all who obey Him, and He was declared by God a high priest in the order of Melchizedek.

J esus, our High Priest, came according to the order of Melchizedek, the priestly king of Salem, which is modern-day Jerusalem. It is

Melchizedek who became Abram's ally in the day when nobody else in all civilization recognized the Most High God. Together, they pointed to God as the victor over a fierce battle in which Abram prevailed against a vast army.

In the Old Testament, the high priest's most important task happened on the Day of Atonement. He made a blood sacrifice to atone for the sins of the congregation and himself. Then he—and only he—was allowed to enter the presence of God in the Holy of Holies and sprinkle the blood on God's "throne"—the mercy seat.

Jesus serves today as our High Priest as He makes the way for us to know the Most High God. Melchizedek lived in the weakness of human flesh and had to make atonement for his own sins. However, Jesus endured the temptation and pain that befalls mankind, but He did not commit any wrong to merit this suffering; rather, God ordained that Jesus suffer as part of a much greater plan—the salvation of all mankind. Jesus, through His obedience, was made perfect through suffering. He is our perfect High Priest.

Earthly priests point us toward God, but it is only through the perfect work of Jesus, our High Priest, that we can have eternal salvation and be united with God.

1 Corinthians 1:1–9
God Is Faithful

Paul, called as an apostle of Christ Jesus by God's will, and Sosthenes our brother:

To God's church at Corinth, to those who are sanctified in Christ Jesus and called as saints, with all those in every place who call on the name of Jesus Christ our Lord—both their Lord and ours.

Grace to you and peace from God our Father and the Lord Jesus Christ.

I always thank my God for you because of God's grace given to you in Christ Jesus, that by Him you were enriched in everything—in all speech and all knowledge. In this way, the testimony about Christ was confirmed among you, so that you do not lack any spiritual gift as you eagerly wait for the revelation of our Lord Jesus Christ. He will also strengthen you to the end, so that you will be blameless in the day of our Lord Jesus Christ. God is faithful; you were called by Him into fellowship with His Son, Jesus Christ our Lord.

Old Faithful is a cone geyser that is located in Yellowstone National Park in Wyoming. It is one of the most predictable geographical oddities on the planet, sending boiling water up to 184 feet in the air. The name says it all: it is faithful and can be counted on to keep doing what it's been doing for all these years—erupting with great regularity.

Tourists flock to Old Faithful in droves. There are other geysers in Yellowstone, but Old Faithful is the most famous. Why? Likely because the tourists know that due to its regularity, they'll get to see it blow. Not many other geysers are as predictable. It erupts every 60 to 110 minutes, and staff members can predict the eruptions with amazing accuracy. In fact, about 90 percent of the predicted eruptions for Old Faithful are correct within a window of plus or minus 10 minutes. We humans like something we can count on, and Old Faithful delivers.

The apostle Paul described God as faithful in 1 Corinthians 1:9. He was the faithful One who had called the Corinthians to a saving knowledge of Jesus Christ, and He was the faithful One who bestowed spiritual gifts on the members of the church in Corinth. God was the faithful One who would, by His grace, keep the Corinthian believers "blameless in the day of our Lord Jesus Christ" (v. 8).

One of the great spiritual "aha" moments in our journey with Christ is when we become aware that even if we are not always faithful to the Lord, He remains faithful to us. He is faithful, dependable, and unchanging. He is the most faithful force on the planet—much more so even than Old Faithful.

Old Faithful info came from: http://mms.nps.gov/yell/ofvec/exhibits/eruption/prediction/predict7.htm.

Acts 4:13-21
Compelled to Speak

When they observed the boldness of Peter and John and realized that they were uneducated and untrained men, they were amazed and recognized that they had been with Jesus. And since they saw the man who had been healed standing with them, they had nothing to say in response. After they had ordered them to leave the Sanhedrin, they conferred among themselves, saying, "What should we do with these men? For an obvious sign, evident to all who live in Jerusalem, has been done through them, and we cannot deny it! However, so this does not spread any further among the people, let's threaten them against speaking to anyone in this name again." So they called for them and ordered them not to preach or teach at all in the name of Jesus.

But Peter and John answered them, "Whether it's right in the sight of God for us to listen to you rather than to God, you decide; for we are unable to stop speaking about what we have seen and heard."

After threatening them further, they released them. They found no way to punish them, because the people were all giving glory to God over what had been done.

What are you ready to talk about right now? For some, it's your grandkids. People who have grandchildren don't need much of an opening to talk about how cute and smart they are. For others, it's sports. You might be so excited about the big game your team is about to play in that your Facebook friends are ready to unsubscribe to your posts because they're tired of hearing about it. Others might have trouble staying quiet about negative things—what that annoying co-worker did today, how much you hate your job, or what your husband said to you that really made you angry.

For Peter and John, it was Jesus. They could not stop talking about Him. In fact, they talked about Him so much that the Jewish leaders were tired of hearing about Him. They took Peter and John into custody and threatened them, ordering them not to speak Jesus' name ever again.

It was impossible, though. Peter and John couldn't stop talking about Jesus any more than you can stop talking about your sweet grandbaby or favorite team. They wouldn't even pretend they could, and they let the religious leaders know it up front. They were compelled to tell people about Jesus, because Jesus was their greatest love, blessing, and priority in life.

Is He that for you? Is Jesus such a big part of your life that you can't help but talk about Him and how much He loves you and you love Him? We often want to talk about the things we think about the most. Let's strive to think more on things above so that we can't keep from speaking about things that matter in eternity.

1 Corinthians 15:24–28
Promise of Final Victory

Then comes the end, when He hands over the kingdom to God the Father, when He abolishes all rule and all authority and power. For He must reign until He puts all His enemies under His feet. The last enemy to be abolished is death. For God has put everything under His feet. But when it says "everything" is put under Him, it is obvious that He who puts everything under Him is the exception. And when everything is subject to Christ, then the Son Himself will also be subject to the One who subjected everything to Him, so that God may be all in all.

Death is a stark, and sometimes dark, reminder that we live in a fallen world. Most of us have faced the reality of death through the loss of a loved one or dear friend. Eventually, we will face it ourselves. Death is inevitable. We were born to die.

We have made attempts to forestall death. Medical science advancements have resulted in cures for many diseases that in earlier human history led to the death of thousands. We are grateful for these advances, but in the long run, all attempts to avert death will fail. That is, except one. Through Christ's resurrection, all enemies of the Lord have been vanquished, including the greatest enemy of all—death.

A father and son were driving down the highway one day with the windows down when the child began screaming. The dad spotted a honeybee flying inside the car and began slowing down. His child was allergic to bee stings and doctors had warned that the next one could be fatal. As the father pulled the car onto the side of the road, he reached out and grabbed the bee out of the air.

Killing the motor, he turned to his son, held out his hand, and opened his palm. As soon as he saw the bee, the little boy began crying again. Why would his dad put him in harm's way again? But the father said, "Look in my hand, son. There is his stinger. That bee cannot ever hurt anyone again."

In 1 Corinthians 15:55, the apostle Paul taunts death. "Death, where is your victory? Death, where is your sting?" Like the honeybee without his stinger, death is still flying around frightening people, but for all who are in Christ, death has lost its sting.

By His own death, Jesus paid the price to redeem us from death and the grave. By His resurrection, He conquered death and gave us the victory. Yes, physical death still will come to us all (unless the Lord returns first). However, death is not the end for believers in Christ, but rather a transition into the presence of the Lord, where we will live in heaven forever and ever.

· Romans 4:13-25
Not by the Law

For the promise to Abraham or to his descendants that he would inherit the world was not through the law, but through the righteousness that comes by faith. If those who are of the law are heirs, faith is made empty and the promise is canceled. For the law produces wrath. And where there is no law, there is no transgression.

This is why the promise is by faith, so that it may be according to grace, to guarantee it to all the descendants—not only to those who are of the law but also to those who are of Abraham's faith. He is the father of us all in God's sight. As it is written: I have made you the father of many nations. He believed in God, who gives life to the dead and calls things into existence that do not exist. He believed, hoping against hope, so that he became the father of many nations according to what had been spoken: So will your descendants be. He considered his own body to be already dead (since he was about 100 years old) and also considered the deadness of Sarah's womb, without weakening in the faith. He did not waver in unbelief at God's promise but was strengthened in his faith and gave glory to God, because he was fully convinced that what He had promised He was also able to perform. Therefore, it was credited to him for righteousness. Now it was credited to him was not written for Abraham alone, but also for us. It will be credited to us who believe in Him who raised Jesus our Lord from the dead. He was delivered up for our trespasses and raised for our justification.

When asked the difference between Christianity and all other religions, a prominent preacher answered by saying, "You spell all other religions DO. You spell Christianity DONE." All religions except Christianity require the believer to meet the requirements of righteousness through religious acts and habits—you must DO certain things to earn your way into heaven. In Christianity, God has DONE all that is required for us to be righteous and to have eternal life through His Son, Jesus Christ.

Paul said essentially the same thing when he wrote to the Christians in Rome. To paraphrase: "If you earn your righteousness by doing religious things recorded in the Law, then your trust in what God has done in Christ Jesus is null and void." The promise of an eternal relationship with God comes through repenting and believing in what God has done, not in what we can do to earn it. If we try to earn it through our works, we are saying that what Jesus did on the cross wasn't good enough.

Have you put your complete trust in all that God has done in Jesus Christ to secure for you salvation and eternal life?

1 John 1:1–10
A Spiritual Audit

What was from the beginning, what we have heard, what we have seen with our eyes, what we have observed and have touched with our hands, concerning the Word of life—that life was revealed, and we have seen it and we testify and declare to you the eternal life that was with the Father and was revealed to us—what we have seen and heard we also declare to you, so that you may have fellowship along with us; and indeed our fellowship is with the Father and with His Son Jesus Christ. We are writing these things so that our joy may be complete.

Now this is the message we have heard from Him and declare to you: God is light, and there is absolutely no darkness in Him. If we say, "We have fellowship with Him," yet we walk in darkness, we are lying and are not practicing the truth. But if we walk in the light as He Himself is in the light, we have fellowship with one another, and the blood of Jesus His Son cleanses us from all sin. If we say, "We have no sin," we are deceiving ourselves, and the truth is not in us. If we confess our sins, He is faithful and righteous to forgive us our sins and to cleanse us from all unrighteousness. If we say, "We don't have any sin," we make Him a liar, and His word is not in us.

Tax season can be a stressful time for many of us. We have to gather our forms and receipts, and document our assets and liabilities. Every digit counts when the accountant begins claiming, deducting, and itemizing. We shudder at the thought of an audit. Even if we think we've done it all right, we're never quite sure, and the idea of having to drag out all of those old statements, receipts, and returns can be overwhelming.

Wouldn't we be surprised if we received a letter stating we had been flagged to be audited spiritually? How would we respond? Would we scramble around gathering old prayer journals, baptism certificates, and giving records? Would we wonder if we'd done it right? Or would we have a terrible pit in our stomach, knowing that we *didn't* do it right? Of course, the idea of a spiritual audit isn't real, but it should cause us to think!

God's Word tells us there is an audit of sorts, performed by the Holy Spirit. If we claim to live in the light, the proof is in our staying away from darkness, experiencing fellowship with God and each other, and being cleansed from sin by the blood of Jesus. By claiming we have no sin, we essentially call God a liar.

Is the Holy Spirit knocking at your heart's door? Is it time for an audit? Own up to your sins, confess them, receive forgiveness, and let God cleanse you "from all unrighteousness."

Acts 8:26–35
Guides Needed

An angel of the Lord spoke to Philip: "Get up and go south to the road that goes down from Jerusalem to Gaza." (This is the desert road.) So he got up and went. There was an Ethiopian man, a eunuch and high official of Candace, queen of the Ethiopians, who was in charge of her entire treasury. He had come to worship in Jerusalem and was sitting in his chariot on his way home, reading the prophet Isaiah aloud.

The Spirit told Philip, "Go and join that chariot."

When Philip ran up to it, he heard him reading the prophet Isaiah, and said, "Do you understand what you're reading?"

"How can I," he said, "unless someone guides me?" So he invited Philip to come up and sit with him. Now the Scripture passage he was reading was this: He was led like a sheep to the slaughter, and as a lamb is silent before its shearer, so He does not open His mouth. In His humiliation justice was denied Him. Who will describe His generation? For His life is taken from the earth.

The eunuch replied to Philip, "I ask you, who is the prophet saying this about—himself or another person?" So Philip proceeded to tell him the good news about Jesus, beginning from that Scripture.

A teenage girl was being bullied at school. She had approached her parents about it, but they told her to just stand up to the bullies and not let them win. They didn't give her any strategies to help her do this, and they weren't believers, so they couldn't give her any spiritual guidance. She became more and more withdrawn, and she was spiraling into a deep depression when her aunt came to visit.

The aunt could tell something was wrong, and she got her niece to open up to her. The girl admitted she was at the end of her rope and didn't know what to do. Then the aunt was able to share the good news of Jesus with her niece. Once the girl had the hope of Jesus, her aunt was able to help guide her through the process of dealing with the bullies on not just an emotional level but also a spiritual one.

People everywhere are seeking answers. Having someone to walk with us through life's difficulties, answering our questions and encouraging us along the way, is indeed a blessing. Philip became a guide for the Ethiopian in his search for truth. Philip was able to do so because he had responded obediently to the angel of the Lord (vv. 26–27) and followed the Holy Spirit's leading (v. 29). Philip could lead the Ethiopian because he was being guided by the Spirit.

Under the leadership of the Holy Spirit, divine encounters are possible every day. They are not always obvious, so we need to be sensitive to the Spirit's leading and keep our eyes open for those who may be hurting or searching. Are you willing to be a guide He can use?

Philippians 3:10–17
Eyes on the Prize

*My goal is to know Him and the power of His res-
urrection and the fellowship of His sufferings, being
conformed to His death, assuming that I will somehow reach the resurrection from among the dead.*

*Not that I have already reached the goal or
am already fully mature, but I make every effort
to take hold of it because I also have been taken
hold of by Christ Jesus. Brothers, I do not consider
myself to have taken hold of it. But one thing I do:
Forgetting what is behind and reaching forward
to what is ahead, I pursue as my goal the prize
promised by God's heavenly call in Christ Jesus.
Therefore, all who are mature should think this way.
And if you think differently about anything, God
will reveal this also to you. In any case, we should
live up to whatever truth we have attained. Join in
imitating me, brothers, and observe those who live
according to the example you have in us.*

Have you ever watched a triathlon? The athletes that choose to
participate in the swimming, biking, and running competition
are serious about their task. Most of them know they're not going to
win, but they compete anyway. They do it for the satisfaction of setting
a very lofty goal and attaining it. And they don't just decide to do it on
the day of competition. That would be lunacy. It would be impossible

to just jump in with no preparation and expect to succeed; they would fall far short of their goal. Therefore, there is much training involved. The athletes prepare for the race both physically and mentally. They acquire the proper clothing and gear that will best help them reach their goal of the finish line.

During the race itself, the athletes are focused. They don't turn to wave at the fans, stop to gaze at the pretty clouds, or take a break. They fix their sights on where they're going next, not where they've already been. There's no point in going back or even looking back; it would only detract from their goal of the finish line. They continue on to their goal with focused determination, and when they reach the end, there is celebration!

In writing to the Philippians, Paul borrowed the language of the sportsperson and compared the life of a Christian to that of an athlete who trains to compete. As believers, we can model the athlete's complete focus and energy, fixed on that goal of knowing Christ and being more like Him.

Maybe our days of serious athletic competition are past (or maybe we never were the athletic type). But we can all be like athletes in setting aside any distractions and pursuing Christ as our first priority. With our eyes fixed on Jesus, we can be champions in running the race of the Christian life. And when we reach the end of our earthly lives, there will be a celebration unlike any we can experience on Earth.

1 Peter 2:11–17
Good Citizens

*Dear friends, I urge you as strangers and tempo-
rary residents to abstain from fleshly desires that
war against you. Conduct yourselves honorably
among the Gentiles, so that in a case where they
speak against you as those who do what is evil,
they will, by observing your good works, glorify God
on the day of visitation.*

*Submit to every human authority because of
the Lord, whether to the Emperor as the supreme
authority or to governors as those sent out by him
to punish those who do what is evil and to praise
those who do what is good. For it is God's will
that you silence the ignorance of foolish people by
doing good. As God's slaves, live as free people,
but don't use your freedom as a way to conceal
evil. Honor everyone. Love the brotherhood. Fear
God. Honor the Emperor.*

Being a good citizen has absolutely nothing to do with politics. A
good citizen can be apolitical or even despise everything that goes
on in the government. Citizenship has to do with self-respect, duty,
responsibility, submission to authorities, and honorable living.

What does this have to do with God? The apostle Peter writes
in his first epistle, "For it is God's will that you silence the ignorance
of foolish people by doing good" (1 Pet. 2:15). When we do what we

are supposed to do—our civic duty, one might say—we demonstrate that we understand and accept the laws of God. When we have honest conversations with lost people, we are able to translate this knowledge into the precepts of God.

In other words, when we are good citizens, it gives us the credibility to share the gospel with others. If we break the laws of the land, such as theft, or murder, or even speeding or texting while driving, we look like everyone else and have lost our witness. Why would anyone want to follow our God if doing so doesn't seem to make any difference in the way we live our lives? But if we live honorably, those who do not follow Christ will see our good works and it will cause them to glorify God.

We are called out of lostness into holiness. Everything about us—everything we say and everything we do—must be intentional to bring the Light of Jesus Christ into a dark and dying world. Our actions matter so much, not just because we are called to be obedient to God, but because those actions speak volumes to the world about the One we follow. Let's honor Him by saying and doing things that will make others want to follow Him as well!

James 1:2–12
Becoming Mature Through Adversity

Consider it a great joy, my brothers, whenever you experience various trials, knowing that the testing of your faith produces endurance. But endurance must do its complete work, so that you may be mature and complete, lacking nothing.

Now if any of you lacks wisdom, he should ask God, who gives to all generously and without criticizing, and it will be given to him. But let him ask in faith without doubting. For the doubter is like the surging sea, driven and tossed by the wind. That person should not expect to receive anything from the Lord. An indecisive man is unstable in all his ways.

The brother of humble circumstances should boast in his exaltation, but the one who is rich should boast in his humiliation because he will pass away like a flower of the field. For the sun rises with its scorching heat and dries up the grass; its flower falls off, and its beautiful appearance is destroyed. In the same way, the rich man will wither away while pursuing his activities.

A man who endures trials is blessed, because when he passes the test he will receive the crown of life that God has promised to those who love Him.

In a jail cell she awaits her trial. She was arrested for keeping ten children's Bibles at her nursery school. Steadfast in her faith, she ponders her prison term with one guarantee—God is present with her and will give her the strength to endure.

A man heads home in his car with his personal effects in a box in the back seat. He refused to do something he thought was unethical, so his boss fired him. He thinks about his wife and three kids at home, and he wonders how he will support them now, but he is choosing not to worry about it. He knows that God has provided for his family in the past, and He will continue to do so. The man is actually even a little bit excited to see what God will do next.

James addresses his letter to the Jewish Christians who live outside of Palestine, scattered abroad. James exhorts these believers to view each trial with joy versus dismay. Trials serve as an opportunity to grow and mature as a believer's faith is tested by everyday human events, even persecution.

Is it possible that joy and trials can coexist? James tells us that as we press through times of trial, we emerge with stronger faith and character. Though we are tempted to rail against trials, question God, and worry ourselves sick, we can choose instead to grow in patience and endurance. Patience in our heart allows us to develop the wholeness of a mature spiritual journey. Jesus exemplifies perseverance under trial, thus we look to Him for strength and joy in our times of stress.

2 Corinthians 12:5–10
The Strength of Weakness

I will boast about this person, but not about myself, except of my weaknesses. For if I want to boast, I will not be a fool, because I will be telling the truth. But I will spare you, so that no one can credit me with something beyond what he sees in me or hears from me, especially because of the extraordinary revelations. Therefore, so that I would not exalt myself, a thorn in the flesh was given to me, a messenger of Satan to torment me so I would not exalt myself. Concerning this, I pleaded with the Lord three times to take it away from me. But He said to me, "My grace is sufficient for you, for power is perfected in weakness." Therefore, I will most gladly boast all the more about my weaknesses, so that Christ's power may reside in me. So I take pleasure in weaknesses, insults, catastrophes, persecutions, and in pressures, because of Christ. For when I am weak, then I am strong.

Sitting in his front room, head hung down in discouragement, he cried out to God. A competent and confident leader accustomed to finding solutions, his situation was bigger than he could handle. The words came haltingly, "God, I just can't do this any more. I'm at the end of my rope. Unless You intervene, there is no hope." Sitting there for a few more minutes, he sighed, got up, and left for the day.

With a wife and three children and the demands of a fruitful career, his life was full, but manageable. The sudden death of his mother and added responsibility to care for his paralyzed father pressed heavily upon him. He knew he could not continue to deal with it all in his own strength. He needed God's help.

We've all been in similar circumstances where our strength waned. For Paul, it was an infirmity of the flesh. For some, it is the death of a family member or a close friend. For others, it is the burden of broken relationships. For many, it is the weight of financial uncertainty. But, for all, the Lord's Word is a welcomed relief: "My grace is sufficient."

Often, we forget to ask God for help until we've exhausted all of our own strength. The man's prayer above illustrates this. He had tried to do it on his own, but he had failed. Whether it's simply a part of the human condition or a result of our individualistic Western society, reliance upon self to deal with our problems is not a biblical solution. We need to admit our weaknesses—even take pleasure in them, as Paul did—because God's strength is all the more evident when we are weak. His grace is sufficient, and His strength is sufficient for all of us.

Acts 11:19–26
Labeled for Life

Those who had been scattered as a result of the persecution that started because of Stephen made their way as far as Phoenicia, Cyprus, and Antioch, speaking the message to no one except Jews. But there were some of them, Cypriot and Cyrenian men, who came to Antioch and began speaking to the Hellenists, proclaiming the good news about the Lord Jesus. The Lord's hand was with them, and a large number who believed turned to the Lord. Then the report about them was heard by the church that was at Jerusalem, and they sent out Barnabas to travel as far as Antioch. When he arrived and saw the grace of God, he was glad and encouraged all of them to remain true to the Lord with a firm resolve of the heart, for he was a good man, full of the Holy Spirit and of faith. And large numbers of people were added to the Lord. Then he went to Tarsus to search for Saul, and when he found him he brought him to Antioch. For a whole year they met with the church and taught large numbers. The disciples were first called Christians at Antioch.

L abels can be helpful if they accurately describe the contents of what is inside. If we went to the grocery store, and none of the containers had labels on them, we'd be in trouble. We would have a hard time figuring out what was inside many of them and would have some big surprises when mealtime came around. But when the package says what's inside, we can be pretty confident of what we're going to get.

At Antioch the followers of Jesus Christ were first labeled as Christians. This happened as a result of the missionary efforts of Barnabas, who first taught the church its purpose and encouraged them to hold tightly to the Lord. Later he found Saul, a former persecutor of the church, and brought him to Antioch to disciple him in the ways of Christ.

Apparently Barnabas did such a good job in discipling the believers in Antioch that they looked like Christ in the way they lived and related to others. This name was given to the followers of Christ first by those who were outside the faith. They meant it as a term of derision, but the Christians wore it proudly because the label accurately described the contents. You knew what you were going to get with a Christian—someone who followed Christ and told others about Him in both word and deed.

Sometimes things and people get mislabeled. The question is not whether you have been labeled, but whether you have been labeled accurately. If being labeled as a Christian means you are living like Jesus and telling others about Him, then wear that label proudly!

1 Timothy 6:9–16
Fight the Good Fight

But those who want to be rich fall into temptation, a trap, and many foolish and harmful desires, which plunge people into ruin and destruction. For the love of money is a root of all kinds of evil, and by craving it, some have wandered away from the faith and pierced themselves with many pains.

But you, man of God, run from these things, and pursue righteousness, godliness, faith, love, endurance, and gentleness. Fight the good fight for the faith; take hold of eternal life that you were called to and have made a good confession about in the presence of many witnesses.

In the presence of God, who gives life to all, and of Christ Jesus, who gave a good confession before Pontius Pilate, I charge you to keep the command without fault or failure until the appearing of our Lord Jesus Christ. God will bring this about in His own time. He is the blessed and only Sovereign, the King of kings, and the Lord of lords, the only One who has immortality, dwelling in unapproachable light; no one has seen or can see Him, to Him be honor and eternal might. Amen.

What would you consider to be a good fight? Some people think a professional boxing match with lots of entertaining twists and turns is a good fight. Others have the opinion that a fight is good if it ends with a surprising knockout punch. These perspectives are valid, but a Christian's fighting "the good fight of faith" has nothing to do with entertainment.

Timothy served in a setting in which some believers had become distracted. Avoiding the temptation to be just as distracted would put Timothy in the throes of a spiritual fight. In the clash, an eagerness to walk in the path of selfish desires would be set against a steady walk of sincere faith in and obedience to Christ. "The good fight" would require that Timothy defend the truth and choose Christlike behaviors, attitudes, and habits. Paul assured Timothy the fight would be worthwhile.

Christ set the example of this fight for us. He came to fulfill a purpose that was worthwhile, one set by His Father. We likewise should seek to accomplish all that the Lord has for our lives. What is the good fight of faith that God has called you to?

First Timothy 1:5 says, "Now the goal of our instruction is love that comes from a pure heart, a good conscience, and a sincere faith." This is what we are called to pursue: righteousness, godliness, faith, love, perseverance, and gentleness. This is the fruit of the Spirit that will see us through to the end.

Every day growing believers faithfully step up and fight against the temptation to be distracted from our commitment to the Lord. And today is no exception.

James 1:12–18
The Source of Good

A man who endures trials is blessed, because when he passes the test he will receive the crown of life that God has promised to those who love Him.

No one undergoing a trial should say, "I am being tempted by God." For God is not tempted by evil, and He Himself doesn't tempt anyone. But each person is tempted when he is drawn away and enticed by his own evil desires. Then after desire has conceived, it gives birth to sin, and when sin is fully grown, it gives birth to death.

Don't be deceived, my dearly loved brothers. Every generous act and every perfect gift is from above, coming down from the Father of lights; with Him there is no variation or shadow cast by turning. By His own choice, He gave us a new birth by the message of truth so that we would be the firstfruits of His creatures.

John Piper has a good word about temptation: "Darkness comes. In the middle of it, the future looks blank. The temptation to quit is huge. Don't. You are in good company. . . . You will argue with yourself that there is no way forward. But with God, nothing is impossible. He has more ropes and ladders and tunnels out of pits than you can conceive. Wait. Pray without ceasing. Hope."

Temptation has a funny way of disguising sin. It can make sin look gloriously exciting. It can make the right thing look terribly dull. Then, you throw pride into the equation—*I don't want to look like a loser*—and choosing to give in to temptation becomes easier.

But stay strong. You are His!

The Bible tells us everyone, even Jesus, has been tempted. Hebrews 2:18 and 4:15 also says we will never be tempted beyond our ability to resist. God will provide a way of escape (1 Cor. 10:13).

James concludes his instructions for Christians when facing trials or temptations with, "Every generous act and every perfect gift is from above . . ." (1:17). Had he ended his explanation at verse 14, the author could have led many Christians into a confusing state that would cause them to straddle the line between faith and works.

In fact, James lays out his instruction in such a way that it is in complete concordance with the gospel of Jesus Christ. This life is hard, but we should remain steadfast. We are unwise, and we should, therefore, ask God for wisdom. We are vulnerable to temptation. Temptation leads to sin, and sin brings about death. Works-based religion agrees with all of these points. However, they lack the climax of this passage, which is what allows Christians to follow Christ faithfully.

If Jesus did not awaken our hearts and provide a transforming faith in us, then all of the above would be impossible to keep. That is the gift—Jesus. He is unchanging and has promised to make us new creatures.

Piper quote: Lilian Kwan, "John Piper Reflects on 30-Year Ministry," *The Christian Post*, December 11, 2012, http://www.christianpost.com/news/john-piper-reflects-on-30-year-ministry-warns-pastors-to-avoid-stereotypes-86491.

Acts 16:22–34
Jail Break

Then the mob joined in the attack against them, and the chief magistrates stripped off their clothes and ordered them to be beaten with rods. After they had inflicted many blows on them, they threw them in jail, ordering the jailer to keep them securely guarded. Receiving such an order, he put them into the inner prison and secured their feet in the stocks.

About midnight Paul and Silas were praying and singing hymns to God, and the prisoners were listening to them. Suddenly there was such a violent earthquake that the foundations of the jail were shaken, and immediately all the doors were opened, and everyone's chains came loose. When the jailer woke up and saw the doors of the prison open, he drew his sword and was going to kill himself, since he thought the prisoners had escaped.

But Paul called out in a loud voice, "Don't harm yourself, because all of us are here!"

Then the jailer called for lights, rushed in, and fell down trembling before Paul and Silas. Then he escorted them out and said, "Sirs, what must I do to be saved?"

So they said, "Believe on the Lord Jesus, and you will be saved—you and your household." Then they spoke the message of the Lord to him along with everyone in his house. He took them the same hour of the night and washed their wounds. Right away he and all his family were baptized. He brought them into his house, set a meal before them, and rejoiced because he had believed God with his entire household.

At most community swimming pools, lifeguards are a fixture. We depend on them to enforce the safety rules (no pushing, no running, no horseplay, no diving in the shallow end) and perhaps to even save a life. In today's verses, we see a word picture of someone being saved—not from drowning, but saved from spiritual death to eternal life.

Paul and Silas found themselves in jail because the city was in an uproar over their preaching. Most recently, some were upset because the two men had driven demons out of a slave girl who had made a living for her owners by telling fortunes. She was no longer of any use to them, and they had lost a source of income. They were furious! A mob joined in, and Paul and Silas were tossed in jail.

But instead of complaining about their unfortunate fate, the two men prayed and sang praises to God. This wasn't quiet humming under their breath. The other prisoners heard the songs. Then a foundation-shaking earthquake erupted and the prison doors broke open. The jailer feared for his life, worried that all the prisoners had escaped. But seeing that Paul and Silas had not escaped, he asked that life-changing question: "What must I do to be saved?" (v. 30).

Salvation comes by believing on the Lord Jesus Christ. Joy came to the jailer and his whole family as they believed in Jesus. Do you know someone who needs to be saved to eternal life? Don't be afraid to tell them!

1 John 4:7-16
An Expression of Love

Dear friends, let us love one another, because love is from God, and everyone who loves has been born of God and knows God. The one who does not love does not know God, because God is love. God's love was revealed among us in this way: God sent His One and Only Son into the world so that we might live through Him. Love consists in this: not that we loved God, but that He loved us and sent His Son to be the propitiation for our sins. Dear friends, if God loved us in this way, we also must love one another. No one has ever seen God. If we love one another, God remains in us and His love is perfected in us.

This is how we know that we remain in Him and He in us: He has given assurance to us from His Spirit. And we have seen and we testify that the Father has sent His Son as the world's Savior. Whoever confesses that Jesus is the Son of God— God remains in him and he in God. And we have come to know and to believe the love that God has for us. God is love, and the one who remains in love remains in God, and God remains in him.

The apostle John spent a lot of time encouraging his reader by giving proofs of salvation. Loving one another is a proof of the indwelling of the Holy Spirit, and this is proof of true belief in Jesus.

Have you ever noticed how simple the code of living the Christian life really is? Love God and love your neighbor (see Mark 12:30–31). Every action is an expression of the love of something. We are either loving God, our neighbor, or ourselves. Even if our actions are often proof of self-love, the longer we know the Lord, the more we'll do things out of love for God and our neighbor. This is a good and clear proof that the Holy Spirit is at work. We cannot love this way except that God first took the initiative in loving us. This love empowers us to love one another just as God loves us.

A husband/wife couple serves as doctors in a hospital located in desperately poor surroundings. Earnestly, they perform heroic measures to save the lives of malformed and malnourished infants. The doctors work full days and then respond to calls at night, all to rescue young babies from the clutches of death. The hospital, though limited in resources, has declared that it will not turn away a single patient in need of care.

Like these doctors, our Great Physician has no deeper wish than to save mankind. No person is turned away from His free offer of salvation. The Father sent His only Son for us, and Jesus' love compelled Him to give the ultimate sacrificial gift, His very life. May we join Him in offering this lifesaving message to all who are perishing.

Hebrews 10:19–25
Never Give Up

*Therefore, brothers, since we have boldness
to enter the sanctuary through the blood of Jesus,
by a new and living way He has opened for us
through the curtain (that is, His flesh), and since we
have a great high priest over the house of God, let
us draw near with a true heart in full assurance of
faith, our hearts sprinkled clean from an evil conscience and our bodies washed in pure water. Let
us hold on to the confession of our hope without
wavering, for He who promised is faithful. And let
us be concerned about one another in order to
promote love and good works, not staying away
from our worship meetings, as some habitually do,
but encouraging each other, and all the more as
you see the day drawing near.*

In 1941, British Prime Minister Winston Churchill gave a speech
to the students at Harrow School in London. Urban legend reports
that all he said was, "Never give up. Never, never, never give up,"
before sitting down. However, the truth is he gave a full speech, and
it included a section on not giving in. The text reads: "Never give in.
Never give in. Never, never, never—in nothing, great or small, large or
petty—never give in, except to convictions of honour and good sense.
Never yield to force. Never yield to the apparently overwhelming might
of the enemy."

Several decades later, while suffering from cancer, college basketball coach and broadcaster Jim Valvano gave his famous ESPY speech that was highlighted by the exhortation, "Don't give up . . . don't ever give up!" He explained, "Cancer can take away all of my physical abilities. It cannot touch my mind, it cannot touch my heart, and it cannot touch my soul." Valvano died just eight weeks after that night.

The writer of Hebrews had a similar message to that of these two men. For those in Christ, there are some things that no circumstance, trial, situation, or difficulty can ever touch. Most importantly, sin cannot touch the assurance of forgiveness that we have through the perfect sacrifice of Jesus Christ.

It may sound odd, but our confidence comes because there's nothing we can do to change the situation. There is no sacrifice we can make for God to accept us more than He already does because of the cross. If we give up on Jesus, we have no hope. So we should hold tight to the faith we profess. With God's help, we can resist the enemy and hold on to what we know is true. God keeps His promises. Don't give in . . . don't ever give in!

Churchill quote: http://www.school-for-champions.com/speeches/churchill_never_give_in.htm#.VyOg75MrJE4.

Valvano quote: http://www.jimmyv.org/about-us/remembering-jim/jimmy-v-espy-awards-speech.

2 Timothy 3:1–14
Watch the Company You Keep

But know this: Difficult times will come in the last days. For people will be lovers of self, lovers of money, boastful, proud, blasphemers, disobedient to parents, ungrateful, unholy, unloving, irreconcilable, slanderers, without self-control, brutal, without love for what is good, traitors, reckless, conceited, lovers of pleasure rather than lovers of God, holding to the form of godliness but denying its power. Avoid these people!

For among them are those who worm their way into households and capture idle women burdened down with sins, led along by a variety of passions, always learning and never able to come to a knowledge of the truth. Just as Jannes and Jambres resisted Moses, so these also resist the truth, men who are corrupt in mind, worthless in regard to the faith. But they will not make further progress, for their lack of understanding will be clear to all, as theirs was also.

But you have followed my teaching, conduct, purpose, faith, patience, love, and endurance, along with the persecutions and sufferings that came to me in Antioch, Iconium, and Lystra. What persecutions I endured! Yet the Lord rescued me from them all. In fact, all those who want to live a godly life in Christ Jesus will be persecuted. Evil people and impostors will become worse, deceiving and being deceived. But as for you, continue in what you have learned and firmly believed.

These are perilous times. Acts of terror and ungodly lifestyles are commonplace. Actors, athletes, politicians, and ordinary people who deny the Bible and seek to follow their own selfish ways are prevalent. It makes you want to be an ostrich with your head in the sand or threaten to move to another country, hoping to avoid all the chaos, but we know we can't—at least until Jesus returns.

Yet, this isn't something new, and it's not just something happening in our own country. Sin abounds everywhere, and it has for all of history. Paul, writing just a few decades after the earthly ministry of Jesus, gave us a list of sinful attributes that could be applied with ease to our own times. We are surrounded by those who would have us believe that there is no God, and that His commandments are trite and no longer meaningful in contemporary society. But Paul, writing under the inspiration of the Holy Spirit, sums up how we are to respond to those who might claim to be believers, but whose lives show no signs of godliness. He simply says in three words, "Avoid these people."

We can't judge our brothers and sisters, but God's Word certainly gives us a measuring rod. Ask God to give you understanding to discern between those who are godly and those who have a form of godliness. Pray for others, and commit to being salt and light in a dark world.

Romans 2:1–10
The Right Focus

Therefore, any one of you who judges is without excuse. For when you judge another, you condemn yourself, since you, the judge, do the same things. We know that God's judgment on those who do such things is based on the truth. Do you really think—anyone of you who judges those who do such things yet do the same—that you will escape God's judgment? Or do you despise the riches of His kindness, restraint, and patience, not recognizing that God's kindness is intended to lead you to repentance? But because of your hardness and unrepentant heart you are storing up wrath for yourself in the day of wrath, when God's righteous judgment is revealed. He will repay each one according to his works: eternal life to those who by persistence in doing good seek glory, honor, and immortality; but wrath and indignation to those who are self-seeking and disobey the truth but are obeying unrighteousness; affliction and distress for every human being who does evil, first to the Jew, and also to the Greek; but glory, honor, and peace for everyone who does what is good, first to the Jew, and also to the Greek.

I t's all about focus. You've probably heard the old saying, "Every time you point a finger in judgment at someone else, you have three fingers pointing back at yourself." Paul goes even further and says it's inexcusable to judge anyone because we all sin. Perhaps your sins are different but sin is sin. In Romans 1, Paul even listed some of those sins that remind us we are all sinners: "They are full of envy, murder, quarrels, deceit, and malice. They are gossips, slanderers, God-haters, arrogant, proud, boastful, inventors of evil, disobedient to parents, undiscerning, untrustworthy, unloving, and unmerciful" (vv. 29–31). He definitely encompassed all of us in that list.

We often have the mistaken notion that if we focus on someone else's sins, we don't have to deal with our own, which is inexcusable. Therefore, the next time we want to make a judgmental remark, we'd be wise to realize while that may not be a sin we struggle with, we all struggle with sin in various forms. That person we're judging could easily judge us on the sin we can't shake but she doesn't have a problem with. We need to get the focus back on our own personal sins and forgiveness—not focus on the sins of others.

In judging, we may unintentionally focus on condemnation and not on God's goodness, which leads to repentance. Conversely, if we focus on God's goodness and grace, we will be less likely to judge others and more likely to repent of our own shortcomings. It's all about focus.

1 Corinthians 9:16-23
Free to Serve

For if I preach the gospel, I have no reason to boast, because an obligation is placed on me. And woe to me if I do not preach the gospel! For if I do this willingly, I have a reward, but if unwillingly, I am entrusted with a stewardship. What then is my reward? To preach the gospel and offer it free of charge and not make full use of my authority in the gospel.

Although I am a free man and not anyone's slave, I have made myself a slave to everyone, in order to win more people. To the Jews I became like a Jew, to win Jews; to those under the law, like one under the law—though I myself am not under the law—to win those under the law. To those who are without that law, like one without the law—not being without God's law but within Christ's law—to win those without the law. To the weak I became weak, in order to win the weak. I have become all things to all people, so that I may by every possible means save some. Now I do all this because of the gospel, so I may become a partner in its benefits.

I f you were in prison, would you purposefully do something that would send you into solitary confinement? That seems crazy, but apparently there are those who have done so. Why? To share the gospel.

There are stories of men who come to know Christ while behind bars and then take on the task of spreading the gospel within their small part of the world. In order to reach all of their prison mates, they must go to all parts of the prison—even solitary confinement. While nobody in solitary can see anyone else, they can often hear each other. So these prison missionaries get themselves sent to solitary in order that they can read Scripture to and pray with the others in hearing distance. They are willing to do what many would not, in order that they can tell people about Jesus.

While not all of us are called to send ourselves to solitary confinement in a prison, we are all commanded to be servants to others that we might win them to Christ. What does that look like?

Perhaps it means we move to a part of our city that might not be as safe or pretty, but where we can live among people who desperately need to hear about the love of Christ. Maybe we ask our Middle Eastern neighbors about their culture and join them in some cultural practices that do not go against what the Bible teaches. There are many ways we can "become like a Jew," as Paul did.

Those of us who are not in prison have a wide world to reach out to. Let's be as bold and courageous as those prisoners who are willing to put themselves into even more dire circumstances in order to reach others for Jesus.

Romans 3:19–26
Bad News, Good News

*Now we know that whatever the law says speaks
to those who are subject to the law, so that every
mouth may be shut and the whole world may
become subject to God's judgment. For no one
will be justified in His sight by the works of the law,
because the knowledge of sin comes through the
law.*

*But now, apart from the law, God's righteous-
ness has been revealed—attested by the Law and
the Prophets—that is, God's righteousness through
faith in Jesus Christ, to all who believe, since there
is no distinction. For all have sinned and fall short
of the glory of God. They are justified freely by
His grace through the redemption that is in Christ
Jesus. God presented Him as a propitiation through
faith in His blood, to demonstrate His righteousness,
because in His restraint God passed over the sins
previously committed. God presented Him to demonstrate His righteousness at the present time, so
that He would be righteous and declare righteous
the one who has faith in Jesus.*

Ask people what the greatest problem in the world is, and you will
get a myriad of answers: the economy, poverty, hunger, greed, or
misused power. But Christians know the main problem in the world is

the problem that has plagued humanity since the Garden of Eden: sin. It is good to know that in heaven there will be no sin, and, therefore, there will be no problems!

Satan is skilled at distracting people from the problem of sin. He keeps people focused on the cares of the world and selfish gain. In fact, sin is an unpopular word in our modern culture. No one wants to be judged by anyone else for their attitudes, actions, or beliefs. Though sin causes many problems in life, many people prefer to blame others for their problems. But, deep in our hearts, God has written a moral law. Even those without the Bible understand that there are certain things that are wrong.

Many people have sat in a doctor's office and heard frightening news that they have cancer. Such bad news shocks us to our core. But the good news is that medical science has advanced so much that many cancers that were previously a death sentence can be treated today. Many cancer survivors live happy and satisfying lives for decades after being treated for this terrible sickness. Hearing bad news does not always mean that there will be a bad ending.

Though sin is always bad news, there is also the good news about Jesus: He loves us and stands ready to forgive us, if we will turn to Him. Jesus came to free people from the power of sin and death, and to rid the world of its pressing problem. His atonement on the cross solved the problem—if only people would repent and believe in Him. We cannot solve the problem with human power. The only solution is to put our faith in Christ, and He'll make all things right again.

Acts 13:42–49
Turn on the Light

As they were leaving, the people begged that these matters be presented to them the following Sabbath. After the synagogue had been dismissed, many of the Jews and devout proselytes followed Paul and Barnabas, who were speaking with them and persuading them to continue in the grace of God.

The following Sabbath almost the whole town assembled to hear the message of the Lord. But when the Jews saw the crowds, they were filled with jealousy and began to oppose what Paul was saying by insulting him.

Then Paul and Barnabas boldly said: "It was necessary that God's message be spoken to you first. But since you reject it and consider yourselves unworthy of eternal life, we now turn to the Gentiles! For this is what the Lord has commanded us: "I have made you a light for the Gentiles to bring salvation to the ends of the earth."

When the Gentiles heard this, they rejoiced and glorified the message of the Lord, and all who had been appointed to eternal life believed. So the message of the Lord spread through the whole region.

According to Albert Einstein, darkness is not the opposite of light; it is the absence of it. The world is dark because of the presence of sin; it is missing Jesus. The light of Christ will dispel darkness wherever it shines.

The Jews were the first to hear the good news about Jesus. However, many rejected the message and vehemently voiced anger at those who proclaimed it. A similar trend is evident in the United States and in many places around the world in this day. Darkness is all around us.

Consequently, it becomes all the more important for those who know Christ to live out our faith openly. Jesus is the Light that shines in darkness. And as witnesses of the Light, He empowers us to be the lights of the world as we reflect His holiness.

People near you are trapped in abject darkness, imprisoned by fear, failure, or folly. Their hearts are hardened and the doors are shut. Our next-door neighbors may need to see the light of Jesus—and we can be that light. Our sons and daughters need to live in the reflection of the light of Jesus in our own lives. We are to be shining examples that make known the good news that anyone can receive salvation; anyone can repent and believe in Christ. We are to be His lights.

Determine to shine so brightly that others will see the Light of Life shining through you and turn to Him. Let the words of Isaiah 9:2 ring true of the people in your life: "The people walking in darkness have seen a great light; a light has dawned on those living in the land of darkness."

Romans 7:13–25
Our Victor

Therefore, did what is good cause my death? Absolutely not! On the contrary, sin, in order to be recognized as sin, was producing death in me through what is good, so that through the commandment, sin might become sinful beyond measure. For we know that the law is spiritual, but I am made out of flesh, sold into sin's power. For I do not understand what I am doing, because I do not practice what I want to do, but I do what I hate. And if I do what I do not want to do, I agree with the law that it is good. So now I am no longer the one doing it, but it is sin living in me. For I know that nothing good lives in me, that is, in my flesh. For the desire to do what is good is with me, but there is no ability to do it. For I do not do the good that I want to do, but I practice the evil that I do not want to do. Now if I do what I do not want, I am no longer the one doing it, but it is the sin that lives in me. So I discover this principle: When I want to do what is good, evil is with me. For in my inner self I joyfully agree with God's law. But I see a different law in the parts of my body, waging war against the law of my mind and taking me prisoner to the law of sin in the parts of my body. What a wretched man I am! Who will rescue me from this dying body? I thank God through

Jesus Christ our Lord! So then, with my mind I myself am a slave to the law of God, but with my flesh, to the law of sin.

Imagine a sporting event where two teams are fighting neck and neck for the victory. The game is tied with only a few minutes left. The crowd wonders how the game will end, until suddenly one of the teams unleashes a secret player with such talent that the ending quickly becomes evident. This player will lead his team to victory.

Throughout Romans, Paul discusses the power of sin and the law and how they both wage war in his body. He cries out with despair over his sin, wondering who can deliver him from the sin warring in his flesh. Then Paul reveals who is the game changer—Jesus Christ. Just as the sports team unleashed its secret player to achieve a victory, God unleashed His plan of redemption for the world and the remedy for sin in Jesus Christ.

Paul reveals it is only Jesus who can defeat the power of sin and death in our bodies. The Lord transforms our hearts and minds that we might have the victory over sin.

1 Thessalonians 5:8–15
Your Encouragement Is Needed

*But since we belong to the day, we must be serious
and put the armor of faith and love on our chests,
and put on a helmet of the hope of salvation. For
God did not appoint us to wrath, but to obtain
salvation through our Lord Jesus Christ, who died
for us, so that whether we are awake or asleep,
we will live together with Him. Therefore encourage
one another and build each other up as you are
already doing.*

*Now we ask you, brothers, to give recogni-
tion to those who labor among you and lead you
in the Lord and admonish you, and to regard
them very highly in love because of their work. Be
at peace among yourselves. And we exhort you,
brothers: warn those who are irresponsible, comfort
the discouraged, help the weak, be patient with
everyone. See to it that no one repays evil for evil
to anyone, but always pursue what is good for one
another and for all.*

A Christian communicator says that whenever she is asked to deliver a message to a church, the person making the request says something to this effect: "We just really need to be encouraged." The interesting thing is, every time that speaker teaches or writes a Bible study, article, devotion, or online blog, she finds herself being encouraged by others. It shouldn't be surprising. That all happens by God's design and for His glory. It is His plan that we find encouragement in one another as we use the gifts He has given us.

Paul did it through letters and teaching the church important truths. He exhorted the Thessalonians not to be anxious about the second coming because believers in Christ are appointed for salvation, not God's wrath. He instructed them to encourage one another until that glorious day.

Jesus is coming again, but life is hard and we need the encouragement of other believers in the meantime. That can happen in a variety of ways, especially as we share our spiritual gifts. So what does it look like for you to be an encourager, using the gifts God has given you?

Perhaps it means you need to mentor someone who is younger in the faith in order to encourage him or her to stand strong and grow in their understanding of God. Maybe it means you send handwritten notes, text messages, or e-mails of encouragement to those you know are struggling with their faith or the circumstances of their lives. It might mean sending a link to a funny article or video to someone who needs some laughter in his life. Or it may mean asking someone out to dinner who needs a break and a chance to relax with a friend. Simply keep an eye out for someone who needs encouragement, and find a way to brighten that person's day and draw them closer to God.

1 Corinthians 12:8–20
A Coordinated Body

To one is given a message of wisdom through the Spirit, to another, a message of knowledge by the same Spirit, to another, faith by the same Spirit, to another, gifts of healing by the one Spirit, to another, the performing of miracles, to another, prophecy, to another, distinguishing between spirits, to another, different kinds of languages, to another, interpretation of languages.

But one and the same Spirit is active in all these, distributing to each person as He wills.

For as the body is one and has many parts, and all the parts of that body, though many, are one body—so also is Christ. For we were all baptized by one Spirit into one body—whether Jews or Greeks, whether slaves or free—and we were all made to drink of one Spirit. So the body is not one part but many. If the foot should say, "Because I'm not a hand, I don't belong to the body," in spite of this it still belongs to the body. And if the ear should say, "Because I'm not an eye, I don't belong to the body," in spite of this it still belongs to the body. If the whole body were an eye, where would the hearing be? If the whole body were an ear, where would the sense of smell be? But now God has placed each one of the parts in one body just as He wanted. And if they were all the same part,

*where would the body be? Now there are many
parts, yet one body.*

Love is a popular theme in music. You can't listen to the radio for
long without hearing a love song (or anti-love song) or two. It's also
difficult to go for long without hearing a song that declares you can't
count on anyone but yourself. It's best to just stick to ourselves and do
our own thing. When we're down, we pick ourselves back up. We can
do it all on our own! Right? Wrong.

The idea that we don't need anyone to improve our situation or to
succeed in life is a popular one, yet an impossibility. To "pull yourself
up by your own bootstraps" is not physically possible. We need one
another in life, and we need one another in the church.

As an eye cannot live and work apart from the body, neither can
we, as members of the body of Christ. We were not only called to salvation to be a child of God, we were called to salvation for a specific task
within community.

As the body of Christ, what is your ordered task? Every part of the
body is important.

You may be an obvious part or you may be a part that is rarely
seen, but each is necessary and significant. Do you consider yourself as
such? Is there anyone you haven't considered as important as yourself?
What changes is the Lord asking you to make in the way you consider
yourself or others?

1 Corinthians 12:21–31
Christian Intimacy

So the eye cannot say to the hand, "I don't need you!" Or again, the head can't say to the feet, "I don't need you!" But even more, those parts of the body that seem to be weaker are necessary. And those parts of the body that we think to be less honorable, we clothe these with greater honor, and our unpresentable parts have a better presentation. But our presentable parts have no need of clothing. Instead, God has put the body together, giving greater honor to the less honorable, so that there would be no division in the body, but that the members would have the same concern for each other. So if one member suffers, all the members suffer with it; if one member is honored, all the members rejoice with it.

Now you are the body of Christ, and individual members of it. And God has placed these in the church: first apostles, second prophets, third teachers, next miracles, then gifts of healing, helping, managing, various kinds of languages. Are all apostles? Are all prophets? Are all teachers? Do all do miracles? Do all have gifts of healing? Do all speak in other languages? Do all interpret?

But desire the greater gifts.

After playing piano for many years, a pianist suffered from carpal tunnel syndrome. When numbness turned to pain and even simple tasks were hindered, she resorted to surgery. Amazed that something so insignificant as a nerve in her wrist could wreak such havoc and impede activity, she was thrilled to be restored to normal function.

Compared to a human body, Paul taught that the church is composed of many members, each indispensable with an important role to fill. Even those whom the world might say are weaker or not honorable are necessary parts of the body and are given greater honor by God. None of us are more important than others in the body of Christ.

Just like when one part of a physical body struggles, and the rest of the body suffers with it in different ways, when one member of Christ's body suffers or struggles, the other members are to share the pain. They are to help restore that one to spiritual health. Just as the pianist never considered amputation to cure her wrist, fellow believers should be so important to us that we strive to keep them vitally connected in our congregations.

Equally significant as shared suffering, however, is shared joy, unimpeded by grudges, envy, or rivalry. How it must bless our Lord when His children take such delight in each other!

Do you consider other believers to be part of the same body as you and realize that the actions and circumstances of each part affects all the others? Do you weep with others' suffering and rejoice with their victories? Remember whose body you are a part of, and strive to live in unity with other believers.

Luke 18:1–8
Pray with Persistence

*He then told them a parable on the need for them
to pray always and not become discouraged:
"There was a judge in a certain town who didn't
fear God or respect man. And a widow in that
town kept coming to him, saying, 'Give me justice
against my adversary.'*

*"For a while he was unwilling, but later he said
to himself, 'Even though I don't fear God or respect
man, yet because this widow keeps pestering me, I
will give her justice, so she doesn't wear me out by
her persistent coming.'"*

*Then the Lord said, "Listen to what the unjust
judge says. Will not God grant justice to His elect
who cry out to Him day and night? Will He delay
to help them? I tell you that He will swiftly grant
them justice. Nevertheless, when the Son of Man
comes, will He find that faith on earth?"*

Luke recorded this parable of Jesus concerning how a persistent
widow influenced a judge to rule fairly in a situation. In the parable, the woman repeatedly made poignant requests for the judge to
help her. Jesus told His disciples that they should, likewise, be persistent in their prayers to God. In the parable, Jesus portrayed the widow
as being a person who appealed to the judge for justice.

Like most parables, there are points at which the analogy can be questioned. After all, humans can't accurately portray God's ways. In this parable, the judge did not believe in God, and he was capable of being worn out. God does not get worn out. Isaiah 40:28 says, "Yahweh is the everlasting God, the Creator of the whole earth. He never grows faint or weary; there is no limit to His understanding." The point of this parable is not that God will give in to us eventually because he gets worn out with hearing our pleas. The point is that we should persist in prayer.

May we pray with confidence that when we ask for God's way and God's will, He will respond. However, note how in the parable, Jesus said the woman repeatedly presented her request to the judge. It wasn't like she asked for justice one day and received the justice that same day. She received an answer only after persistently appealing to the judge.

Why do we sometimes have to pray with persistence? Why doesn't God answer all of our prayers at the same speed? Maybe it's because the timing isn't right. Maybe He wants to teach us something through the process of persistent prayer. Maybe He needs to show us that what we're asking isn't in line with His will. We don't know. The Bible does not provide an exact answer to these questions. However, in this passage in Luke, Jesus instructs us to follow the widow's example of persistent prayer.

2 Corinthians 5:16–21
We Are New People

From now on, then, we do not know anyone in a purely human way. Even if we have known Christ in a purely human way, yet now we no longer know Him in this way. Therefore, if anyone is in Christ, he is a new creation; old things have passed away, and look, new things have come. Everything is from God, who reconciled us to Himself through Christ and gave us the ministry of reconciliation: That is, in Christ, God was reconciling the world to Himself, not counting their trespasses against them, and He has committed the message of reconciliation to us. Therefore, we are ambassadors for Christ, certain that God is appealing through us. We plead on Christ's behalf, "Be reconciled to God." He made the One who did not know sin to be sin for us, so that we might become the righteousness of God in Him.

On the TV show *Extreme Makeover: Home Edition*, homeowners would show Ty Pennington and his team around their houses that were in desperate need of repair and/or didn't meet the needs of the family. Perhaps they needed more rooms, the house might not have been accessible for a family member with a disability, or there may have been structural problems. In many cases it would have been possible to remodel or add on to the existing home, but the crew always decided to restore hope to the family by tearing down the old, damaged home, and building a glorious new one in its place. At the end of the week, the family would walk through their new house, amazed at the difference between the old house and the new. There was no doubt to anyone—the family members or those watching on TV—that this was a brand new house.

Similarly, God doesn't want to just improve our existing lives. Jesus doesn't come to tinker with the original, merely giving it a new façade. Through regeneration, He desires to give us an entirely new identity—to make us into new men and women through and through. A new identity, then, gives birth to a new way of life. Through Christ, we walk, talk, and act in an outward way that demonstrates an inward change. It's amazing what a difference there is between the old person and the new one. There is no doubt to anyone—the believers or those who observe us—that we are brand new people.

When other people look at your life, do they see a different person than they saw before you became a believer? Does the difference Jesus has made in your life make others want to be reconciled to God as well? Do you tell others about the change God has made in your life, and the change He can make in theirs?

Revelation 3:7–13
You Are His

"Write to the angel of the church in Philadelphia:

"The Holy One, the True One, the One who has the key of David, who opens and no one will close, and closes and no one opens says: I know your works. Because you have limited strength, have kept My word, and have not denied My name, look, I have placed before you an open door that no one is able to close. Take note! I will make those from the synagogue of Satan, who claim to be Jews and are not, but are lying—note this—I will make them come and bow down at your feet, and they will know that I have loved you. Because you have kept My command to endure, I will also keep you from the hour of testing that is going to come over the whole world to test those who live on the earth. I am coming quickly. Hold on to what you have, so that no one takes your crown. The victor: I will make him a pillar in the sanctuary of My God, and he will never go out again. I will write on him the name of My God and the name of the city of My God—the new Jerusalem, which comes down out of heaven from My God—and My new name.

"Anyone who has an ear should listen to what the Spirit says to the churches."

The Christians in Philadelphia were obscure, poor, and weak. But they were also faithful to Jesus. John writes that they had kept the Lord's word and had not denied His name. Therefore, Jesus welcomed them in the kingdom with an open door that no one could shut. Moreover, He would let their enemies know that He loved them.

Today, very few may know your name. Your bank account might be unimpressive. In the eyes of the world, you boast very little power. You may never speak in front of thousands or write a best-selling book. In the echelons of government, your authority would only take you to the outer gates of the White House. But if you are a born-again believer, the Creator of the universe knows you by name. He sees your works and opens doors. He loves you.

If you are in Christ, hold on through hardships. Be obedient to His commands. Remain faithful to His name. Stand strong in the face of persecution. Don't be discouraged by a life seemingly lived in the shadows. God sees you.

Jesus supplies strength to the weary. He gives grace to the obedient. He rewards the faithful. He opens a door and welcomes home His own. Will you faithfully endure to the end? Of course you will, because you are His!

Galatians 1:1–12
Only One True Gospel

Paul, an apostle—not from men or by man, but by Jesus Christ and God the Father who raised Him from the dead—and all the brothers who are with me:

To the churches of Galatia.

Grace to you and peace from God the Father and our Lord Jesus Christ, who gave Himself for our sins to rescue us from this present evil age, according to the will of our God and Father. To whom be the glory forever and ever. Amen.

I am amazed that you are so quickly turning away from Him who called you by the grace of Christ and are turning to a different gospel—not that there is another gospel, but there are some who are troubling you and want to change the good news about the Messiah. But even if we or an angel from heaven should preach to you a gospel other than what we have preached to you, a curse be on him! As we have said before, I now say again: If anyone preaches to you a gospel contrary to what you received, a curse be on him!

For am I now trying to win the favor of people, or God? Or am I striving to please people? If I were still trying to please people, I would not be a slave of Christ.

*Now I want you to know, brothers, that the
gospel preached by me is not based on human
thought. For I did not receive it from a human
source and I was not taught it, but it came by a
revelation from Jesus Christ.*

Counterfeiting is an old trade. Throughout history, people interested in exploiting others for their own gain have counterfeited valuable items. One of the greatest counterfeiting capers was by Philadelphia retailer Samuel Upham during the Civil War. He printed fake Confederate bills that could be passed off as actual currency. Upham printed $15 million in fake notes before his crime was discovered.

Throughout history, gospel counterfeits have been presented with surprising frequency. False teachers share novel ideas designed to deceive others. The keys to counterfeiting success are the apparent trustworthiness of the counterfeiter and victims' unfamiliarity with the genuine article. A counterfeiter's goal is to make the product look as similar to the original as possible so that only an expert would be able to tell the difference.

The apostle Paul grieved that Christians in Galatia were tricked by false teachings about the gospel of grace. He warned them to evaluate teaching and teachers, to ensure the one and only gospel was accepted. Today, more than ever, Christians must guard the gospel of Jesus from cheap counterfeits. In order to know the difference, we must be experts in the real gospel. This can only come by studying God's Word. Every word that we hear must be tested against Scripture to see if it is true.

James 2:14–26
Faith with Works

What good is it, my brothers, if someone says he has faith but does not have works? Can his faith save him?

If a brother or sister is without clothes and lacks daily food and one of you says to them, "Go in peace, keep warm, and eat well," but you don't give them what the body needs, what good is it? In the same way faith, if it doesn't have works, is dead by itself.

But someone will say, "You have faith, and I have works." Show me your faith without works, and I will show you faith from my works. You believe that God is one; you do well. The demons also believe—and they shudder.

Foolish man! Are you willing to learn that faith without works is useless? Wasn't Abraham our father justified by works when he offered Isaac his son on the altar? You see that faith was active together with his works, and by works, faith was perfected. So the Scripture was fulfilled that says, Abraham believed God, and it was credited to him for righteousness, and he was called God's friend. You see that a man is justified by works and not by faith alone. And in the same way, wasn't Rahab the prostitute also justified by works when she received

the messengers and sent them out by a differ-
ent route? For just as the body without the spirit is
dead, so also faith without works is dead.

Diagnostic tools and physicians' finely honed skills keep people alive longer today with better life quality than just a few decades ago. Prior to the advent of modern medicine, to determine whether a person was dead, a physician would place a mirror under a patient's nose to see if the person's breath would fog the mirror. If no fog appeared, they would declare that person dead.

James was no physician, but he made it clear that faith has a visible life of its own. The apostle Paul added that God created good works for us as part of His eternal plan (Eph. 2:10). James and his fellow believers often paid a steep price for demonstrating their faith through good works.

Here James explains that our salvation has nothing to do with our works, but our works have everything to do with our salvation. When we surrender our lives to Christ, He begins to live in us in the form of the Holy Spirit. God is good, so good works should come out of our lives when He lives within us. James pulls no punches when he says that if we have no works, then our faith is dead.

Is your faith alive or dead? Let the goodness of God be visible in your life through the good works that you do.

Romans 8:31–39
Love That Cannot Be Defeated

What then are we to say about these things? If God is for us, who is against us? He did not even spare His own Son but offered Him up for us all; how will He not also with Him grant us everything? Who can bring an accusation against God's elect? God is the One who justifies. Who is the one who condemns? Christ Jesus is the One who died, but even more, has been raised; He also is at the right hand of God and intercedes for us. Who can separate us from the love of Christ? Can affliction or anguish or persecution or famine or nakedness or danger or sword?

As it is written: Because of You we are being put to death all day long; we are counted as sheep to be slaughtered. No, in all these things we are more than victorious through Him who loved us. For I am persuaded that not even death or life, angels or rulers, things present or things to come, hostile powers, height or depth, or any other created thing will have the power to separate us from the love of God that is in Christ Jesus our Lord!

Ludwig van Beethoven, though a prolific musical writer, wrote but one opera. Set in the eighteenth century, a man named Florestan suffers unjustly in a Spanish prison. His wife, Leonore, is a noblewoman whose love for Florestan has no bounds. In order to gain access to the prisoners, Leonore disguises herself as an errand boy named Fidelio. Just before Florestan is executed, Leonore finds and rescues her beloved by risking her own life. Leonore loved Florestan so much that she did everything she could to rescue him. She was willing to risk her life for the one she loved.

Similarly, in Romans 8, the apostle Paul characterizes God's love for His children as infinite. Jesus not only risked His life, but He willingly gave His life for us. He rose from the dead and is seated in heaven next to the Father, and He intercedes for us. Nothing can separate us from Him—not death, not spiritual beings, not people who are ruled by evil, not *anything*.

Sometimes life can feel as hard as death. We face threats that come in the form of unfair personal attacks, challenging life circumstances, and constant spiritual warfare. At other times, the Enemy is invisible and threatens us through unknown or unidentified fears. It isn't uncommon to face a combination of challenges that are interpersonal, spiritual, emotional, and physical. There are times when it seems we just cannot win.

But in the midst of all the circumstances of our lives, God's love ensures that we are victors and not victims. Believe God when He says He has made us victors, incapable of ultimate defeat.

Galatians 5:1–13
Live in Freedom

Christ has liberated us to be free. Stand firm then and don't submit again to a yoke of slavery. Take note! I, Paul, tell you that if you get yourselves circumcised, Christ will not benefit you at all. Again I testify to every man who gets himself circumcised that he is obligated to keep the entire law. You who are trying to be justified by the law are alienated from Christ; you have fallen from grace. For through the Spirit, by faith, we eagerly wait for the hope of righteousness. For in Christ Jesus neither circumcision nor uncircumcision accomplishes anything; what matters is faith working through love.

You were running well. Who prevented you from obeying the truth? This persuasion did not come from the One who called you. A little yeast leavens the whole lump of dough. I have confidence in the Lord you will not accept any other view. But whoever it is that is confusing you will pay the penalty. Now brothers, if I still preach circumcision, why am I still persecuted? In that case the offense of the cross has been abolished. I wish those who are disturbing you might also get themselves castrated!

For you were called to be free, brothers.

Years ago, a six-year-old girl was brought to a Christian children's ranch. She was terrified of the world because all she had ever known was neglect and abuse; those who should have loved, protected, and provided for her preferred drugs and the chaotic lifestyle it brought. The children's home provided her a warm bed, plenty of food, clean clothes, and stability. But more importantly, she had new parents who loved her and did everything in their power to make sure the fears of her past had no grounding in her present. They taught her about Jesus and His love for her that exceeded even theirs.

However, when she was a teenager, the girl chose to leave the ranch and return to the cycle of chaos. After all these years, she was still enslaved by the fear that she experienced before she moved to the children's home. She was familiar with fear, and as strange as it sounds, she was comforted by it. But love and trust? Those were uncomfortable for her. It broke her new family's hearts because they simply could not understand how the girl could choose fear over love. She had been set free, yet she went back to the chains of her past.

However, we, too often return to the yoke that enslaved us before Christ saved us. We try to justify ourselves and appease our guilt by following lists of rules. We choose slavery over freedom, guilt over grace. And it breaks His heart. By the grace of God, may we, instead, remember that we are free.

Ephesians 1:1–12
God's Acceptance

Paul, an apostle of Christ Jesus by God's will:

To the faithful saints in Christ Jesus at Ephesus.

Grace to you and peace from God our Father and the Lord Jesus Christ.

Praise the God and Father of our Lord Jesus Christ, who has blessed us in Christ with every spiritual blessing in the heavens. For He chose us in Him, before the foundation of the world, to be holy and blameless in His sight. In love He predestined us to be adopted through Jesus Christ for Himself, according to His favor and will, to the praise of His glorious grace that He favored us with in the Beloved.

We have redemption in Him through His blood, the forgiveness of our trespasses, according to the riches of His grace that He lavished on us with all wisdom and understanding. He made known to us the mystery of His will, according to His good pleasure that He planned in Him for the adminis-tration of the days of fulfillment—to bring everything together in the Messiah, both things in heaven and things on earth in Him.

We have also received an inheritance in Him, predestined according to the purpose of the One who works out everything in agreement with the

decision of His will, so that we who had already
put our hope in the Messiah might bring praise to
His glory.

When Paul wrote to believers at Ephesus, his purpose was to encourage them about the acceptance and inclusion of Gentiles in the church. There were those who questioned the allowance of non-Jews in the early church. Paul strove to combat that position. The imagery he chose here in the letter to the Ephesians was that of adoption: an isolated, cast-aside orphan is chosen, accepted, and made a part of a loving family.

Consider your state before Christ. Whether you were four years old or forty years old when He called you to follow Him, prior to that moment, there was a real and serious division between you and the Father. Like an orphan, you were without a family, with no hope for salvation. There was nothing you could do to earn or position yourself to become part of God's family.

Yet, to the praise of the glory of His grace, the Father has chosen and accepted you. Isn't that amazing news? The acceptance God offers is not based on human performance, but on His own grace. He chooses us because He is good, not because we are. Once He has made us His children, we're a part of His family, not because of our striving or goodness, but because of His grace.

And as His children, we are his heirs. Our inheritance is all of the things God has promised us in salvation that will be reserved for us in heaven. It is an inheritance far beyond any earthly inheritance we could ever be entitled to.

Mark 9:17–27

If

*Out of the crowd, one man answered Him,
"Teacher, I brought my son to You. He has a spirit
that makes him unable to speak. Wherever it
seizes him, it throws him down, and he foams at
the mouth, grinds his teeth, and becomes rigid.
So I asked Your disciples to drive it out, but they
couldn't."*

*He replied to them, "You unbelieving genera-
tion! How long will I be with you? How long must I
put up with you? Bring him to Me."*

*So they brought him to Him. When the spirit
saw Him, it immediately convulsed the boy. He fell
to the ground and rolled around, foaming at the
mouth. "How long has this been happening to him?"
Jesus asked his father.*

*"From childhood," he said. "And many times it
has thrown him into fire or water to destroy him.
But if You can do anything, have compassion on us
and help us."*

*Then Jesus said to him, "'If You can'? Everything
is possible to the one who believes."*

*Immediately the father of the boy cried out, "I
do believe! Help my unbelief."*

*When Jesus saw that a crowd was rapidly com-
ing together, He rebuked the unclean spirit, saying*

*to it, "You mute and deaf spirit, I command you:
come out of him and never enter him again!"*

*Then it came out, shrieking and convulsing him
violently. The boy became like a corpse, so that
many said, "He's dead." But Jesus, taking him by the
hand, raised him, and he stood up.*

The little word *if* is simple to spell. Even though it's a tiny word, it can create problems for us when we use it with God.

"God, if you do this for me, I'll do that for you." "God, if you're so powerful, then make my daughter forgive me." "God, give me a husband, if you can." Do you see how that tiny little word shows that we don't trust God?

The worried father of a troubled child discovered that using *if* complicated his conversation with Jesus. He had brought his child to Jesus' disciples, but they couldn't do anything to help. That's when Jesus showed up and began to talk to him about his child's problem. In the conversation, he implored Jesus to do something *if* He could.

Jesus responded to the frustrated father by calling his *if* into question. The Lord could handle anything. Therefore, no word that implied doubt belonged in the conversation. Only the words *I believe* would suit the situation. Jesus encouraged the man to replace doubt with faith in Him.

Doubt makes us use *if* when we're seeking the Lord's help. Faith compels us to replace it with *I believe*. By trusting the Lord, we can live in the full assurance that nothing we bring to Him will be too tough for Him to handle. Is anything too hard for God?

Ephesians 5:6–20
Get Up, Sleeper!

Let no one deceive you with empty arguments, for God's wrath is coming on the disobedient because of these things. Therefore, do not become their partners. For you were once darkness, but now you are light in the Lord. Walk as children of light—for the fruit of the light results in all goodness, righteousness, and truth—discerning what is pleasing to the Lord. Don't participate in the fruitless works of darkness, but instead expose them. For it is shameful even to mention what is done by them in secret. Everything exposed by the light is made clear, for what makes everything clear is light. Therefore it is said: "Get up, sleeper, and rise up from the dead, and the Messiah will shine on you."

Pay careful attention, then, to how you walk—not as unwise people but as wise—making the most of the time, because the days are evil. So don't be foolish, but understand what the Lord's will is. And don't get drunk with wine, which leads to reckless actions, but be filled by the Spirit: "speaking to one another in psalms, hymns, and spiritual songs, singing and making music from your heart to the Lord, giving thanks always for everything to God the Father in the name of our Lord Jesus Christ."

A sentry has a job to do. In those long, dark stretches of night when everyone else sleeps, he is to remain awake and alert against possible incursions of enemy forces. His job is to protect the people from invasions that may come under cover of night. He is to expose any threats in the darkness. There are many counting on him to do so.

The church has a job to do. We are to "walk as children of light," which will result in "all goodness, righteousness, and truth," as well as wisdom. Unfortunately, in too many instances, we find ourselves nodding off while on duty. Startling us from our complacent reverie, Paul trumpets a reveille in three successive verses—Wake up! Wise up! Walk right!

The days are evil. The Enemy is active. The distractions are many. But God has a plan. His plan is to use us to fulfill His purposes and to reveal His glory. To that end, God calls us to be filled with the Spirit.

The filling of the Spirit is a present-tense command. Though the Holy Spirit came to live in us at the moment of our conversion, we must continually yield ourselves to His fullness through intentional and faithful obedience.

When we abide in the Father, He empowers us to be more than we are. His divine presence enlivens us with vitality and energizes us with strength. We must make the most of the time He gives us and live in His wisdom as we are filled with His Spirit.

Philippians 1:21–30
Prepare the People

For me, living is Christ and dying is gain. Now if I live on in the flesh, this means fruitful work for me; and I don't know which one I should choose. I am pressured by both. I have the desire to depart and be with Christ—which is far better— but to remain in the flesh is more necessary for you. Since I am persuaded of this, I know that I will remain and continue with all of you for your progress and joy in the faith, so that, because of me, your confidence may grow in Christ Jesus when I come to you again.

Just one thing: Live your life in a manner worthy of the gospel of Christ. Then, whether I come and see you or am absent, I will hear about you that you are standing firm in one spirit, with one mind, working side by side for the faith that comes from the gospel, not being frightened in any way by your opponents. This is a sign of destruction for them, but of your deliverance—and this is from God. For it has been given to you on Christ's behalf not only to believe in Him, but also to suffer for Him, having the same struggle that you saw I had and now hear that I have.

We see the T-shirts, signs, mugs, and other memorabilia everywhere: "Baseball is life." "Cheer is life." "Music is life." "Art is life." "Reading is life." "Family is life." We have to wonder if anyone who buys and uses or displays these items really believes what they say. Are any of those things really life? No. They are gross exaggerations— or at least we hope they are. Life is so much more than a sport, a hobby, a career, or even our family.

Paul gave a much more accurate picture of what life is in Philippians 1. Christ is life, and Paul affirmed that Christ is the reason there is life. Apart from Him, life is meaningless. Even if physical life ceases, spiritual life does not. For in death the person who lives in Christ keeps living. He gains life in the eternal presence of God. What could be better than that?

Paul also tells us to "live your life in a manner worthy of the gospel of Christ." Since He is our life, we must live in such a way that we glorify Him. When we do this, we can be united with other believers and stand strong against the enemy.

When people look at your life—the way you spend your time and what you talk about—what would they say it is about? Is it about golf? Is it about your kids? Is it about your job? Is it about entertainment? Those aren't bad things at all. But if your life's focus lies in those things other than in Christ, consider how you might need to change your actions, words, and even thinking so that your life is Christ. Ask God to help you do this today.

Mark 1:1–8
A Spirit of Humility

The beginning of the gospel of Jesus Christ, the Son of God. As it is written in Isaiah the prophet:

Look, I am sending My messenger ahead of You, who will prepare Your way. A voice of one crying out in the wilderness: Prepare the way for the Lord; make His paths straight!*

John came baptizing in the wilderness and preaching a baptism of repentance for the forgiveness of sins. The whole Judean countryside and all the people of Jerusalem were flocking to him, and they were baptized by him in the Jordan River as they confessed their sins. John wore a camel-hair garment with a leather belt around his waist and ate locusts and wild honey. He was preaching: "Someone more powerful than I will come after me. I am not worthy to stoop down and untie the strap of His sandals. I have baptized you with water, but He will baptize you with the Holy Spirit."

John the Baptist was certainly eccentric for his day. He lived in the wilderness, dressed in camel's hair, and ate locusts and wild honey. John also challenged people to be baptized, symbolizing their repentance and the forgiveness of their sins. Because of his radical ideas and lifestyle, some began to wonder if he might be the Messiah. But John, in a spirit of humility, replied that he was not.

Humility is not something that is popular in today's world. Sports figures, music stars, and political candidates all present themselves in the best light possible, bragging to the world about the greatness of their qualities. And it's not just non-Christian celebrities who tout their own accomplishments. A quick glance at social media will reveal a preacher retweeting a compliment or an author posting a glowing review of her latest book. While we're at it, we can't fail to mention the "everyday" people who share a story about their child's deep theological understanding on a subject, post pictures of their vacation with a "So awed by God's creation! #blessed" caption, or otherwise toot their own horn while pretending they're tooting God's. There's even a word for this phenomenon: the humblebrag.

None of us are immune. We all do it. After all, we think, if it's okay for so-and-so celebrity to do it, then it's okay for us. It's what we need to do to succeed in this world. But that's not the way it works. Humility should be the order of the day, even if it means fewer "likes," book sales, or Twitter followers.

John the Baptist, the man whose job it was to tell the world the Messiah was coming—in fact, was here—exhibited a spirit of humility, always understanding that his role was to be one of preparing the way for the Lord. He knew his job was to lift up someone else, not himself.

How would today's world be different if Christians had the same spirit of humility as John the Baptist? What changes would take place in our lives if we pointed people toward the greatness of Jesus rather than pointing to our own achievements?

Acts 4:32–37
Do You Really Need That?

*Now the large group of those who believed were
of one heart and mind, and no one said that any
of his possessions was his own, but instead they
held everything in common. And the apostles were
giving testimony with great power to the resurrection of the Lord Jesus, and great grace was on
all of them. For there was not a needy person
among them, because all those who owned lands
or houses sold them, brought the proceeds of the
things that were sold, and laid them at the apostles' feet. This was then distributed for each person's
basic needs.*

*Joseph, a Levite and a Cypriot by birth, the one
the apostles called Barnabas, which is translated
Son of Encouragement, sold a field he owned,
brought the money, and laid it at the apostles' feet.*

A nd laid them down at the apostles' feet" (v. 35). The church had barely even begun when this happened. At that moment, these Jerusalem Christians were experiencing the Old Testament ideal of Deuteronomy 15:4, "There shall be no poor among you." The tenses in the original text show that this was not a move to become the first Christian commune. Nor was this a rash divesting of all property in immediate expectation of Christ's return. Rather, members voluntarily gave presumably out of either their excess or their sacrificial willingness to downsize so that all might have enough. Acts 4:34 remains a model of voluntary godly giving for the church.

Does this describe today's church? Does it describe your local church? Does it describe you? There's a good chance it doesn't. The kind of giving described in Acts 4 is not very common today. We might think we're generous, but compared to those early believers, most of us aren't. This isn't meant to be a guilt trip. We've been conditioned by our society—and yes, possibly even our churches—to put our own needs first. There are two problems with that mind-set.

First, it's not biblical. We're told to "consider others as more important than yourselves" (Phil. 2:3) and "Love your neighbor as yourself" (Mark 12:31). To put it bluntly, we should not be the most important people in our own lives.

Second, what we think are needs are often just wants. We don't need three cars. We don't need 3,000 feet of living space. We don't need fifteen pairs of shoes. We don't need golf clubs. Or 60-inch TVs. Or five hundred books (even if they are theology books!). You get the picture. Nearly everyone reading this can think of countless things we have but don't really need.

So are we all supposed to sell all of our excess belongings and give that money to the church? That's not what this passage is saying. It's not prescriptive. But when others have needs, and we have the ability to help them, let's consider how we can use our resources to provide aid for those who don't have enough.

Romans 8:1–11
Sink or Swim?

Therefore, no condemnation now exists for those in Christ Jesus, because the Spirit's law of life in Christ Jesus has set you free from the law of sin and of death. What the law could not do since it was limited by the flesh, God did. He condemned sin in the flesh by sending His own Son in flesh like ours under sin's domain, and as a sin offering, in order that the law's requirement would be accomplished in us who do not walk according to the flesh but according to the Spirit. For those who live according to the flesh think about the things of the flesh, but those who live according to the Spirit, about the things of the Spirit. For the mind-set of the flesh is death, but the mind-set of the Spirit is life and peace. For the mind-set of the flesh is hostile to God because it does not submit itself to God's law, for it is unable to do so. Those who are in the flesh cannot please God. You, however, are not in the flesh, but in the Spirit, since the Spirit of God lives in you. But if anyone does not have the Spirit of Christ, he does not belong to Him. Now if Christ is in you, the body is dead because of sin, but the Spirit is life because of righteousness. And if the Spirit of Him who raised Jesus from the dead lives in you, then He who raised Christ from

the dead will also bring your mortal bodies to life
through His Spirit who lives in you.

Name some opposites: hot and cold, love and hate, serious and silly, night and day, short and tall, salt and pepper, up and down, or sink and swim. In today's Scripture passage, Paul named two opposites—life and death—that express totally different extremes. All people fall into one or the other of these mind-sets. Non-believers cannot have God's Spirit living in them. They can never please God, and ultimately their sinful existence, or mind-set, leads to death. But for Christ-followers, with God's Spirit alive in their hearts, there is real life and peace.

This doesn't mean the believer does not die a physical death. Unless Jesus returns before we die, then we will all experience the physical death. But with the Spirit living inside us, we will be raised to eternal life, just as Jesus was raised. With God's Spirit living inside us, we can fully experience God's righteousness and life. The choice sounds simple, yet many people struggle along the road to death, drowning in their sin, when God offers salvation and an abundant life for all who choose it.

So what's it going to be? Sink or swim . . . death or life? God offers life; we must make the choice.

Philippians 4:10–20
The Secret of Being Content

I rejoiced in the Lord greatly that once again you renewed your care for me. You were, in fact, concerned about me but lacked the opportunity to show it. I don't say this out of need, for I have learned to be content in whatever circumstances I am. I know both how to have a little, and I know how to have a lot. In any and all circumstances I have learned the secret of being content—whether well fed or hungry, whether in abundance or in need. I am able to do all things through Him who strengthens me. Still, you did well by sharing with me in my hardship.

And you Philippians know that in the early days of the gospel, when I left Macedonia, no church shared with me in the matter of giving and receiving except you alone. For even in Thessalonica you sent gifts for my need several times. Not that I seek the gift, but I seek the profit that is increasing to your account. But I have received everything in full, and I have an abundance. I am fully supplied, having received from Epaphroditus what you provided—a fragrant offering, an acceptable sacrifice, pleasing to God. And my God will supply all your needs according to His riches in glory in Christ Jesus. Now to our God and Father be glory forever and ever. Amen.

A children's Sunday school class motto is, "I will do the best I can with what I have where I am for Jesus' sake today." That's quite a goal for a young child, but it's what the apostle Paul did. Despite his beatings, harassment, shipwrecks, and alienation from his fellow Jews, he still did his best to spread the gospel of Jesus Christ. And while in prison, Paul wrote to the Philippians saying that no matter what his circumstances were, he had learned to be content. How was He able to do this? Because God strengthened him to do it. And He can do the same for us.

Contentment has to do with attitude—not circumstances. Contentment transcends circumstances and brings an inner sense of peace, even when we are sad, lonely, grieving, and financially challenged. Outwardly, we may suffer, but internally, we can rest assured that the Christ who saved us has also fulfilled His promise to send His Holy Spirit to live within us, to empower us, and to comfort us. He will never leave us nor forsake us.

Believing this promise should spur us on to do the best we can with what we have, where we are, for Jesus' sake today. Not only will contentment make our lives better, but it will also speak volumes to those around us who can't seem to find the contentment that we have. And then we can let them in on our secret to contentment!

Colossians 1:9–20
Redemption in Jesus

For this reason also, since the day we heard this, we haven't stopped praying for you. We are asking that you may be filled with the knowledge of His will in all wisdom and spiritual understanding, so that you may walk worthy of the Lord, fully pleasing to Him, bearing fruit in every good work and growing in the knowledge of God. May you be strengthened with all power, according to His glorious might, for all endurance and patience, with joy giving thanks to the Father, who has enabled you to share in the saints' inheritance in the light. He has rescued us from the domain of darkness and transferred us into the kingdom of the Son He loves. We have redemption, the forgiveness of sins, in Him.

He is the image of the invisible God, the first-born over all creation. For everything was created by Him, in heaven and on earth, the visible and the invisible, whether thrones or dominions or rulers or authorities—all things have been created through Him and for Him. He is before all things, and by Him all things hold together. He is also the head of the body, the church; He is the beginning, the firstborn from the dead, so that He might come to have first place in everything. For God was pleased to have all His fullness dwell in Him, and through

Him to reconcile everything to Himself by making peace through the blood of His cross—whether things on earth or things in heaven.

When Captain Scott O'Grady's F-16 was shot down over Bosnia in June 1995, a search-and-rescue mission was launched immediately. For six days, he evaded opposition forces before he was rescued and brought safely to his ship and the protection of his country. That rescue mission was one of many the United States military has made over the years to save downed pilots and bring them from behind enemy lines into the protective zone of its authority.

When Paul wrote to the Christians in Colossae and encouraged them to praise God, he had the ultimate rescue mission in mind. Like a pilot who is rescued by his commanding officer, we, too, have been rescued from "the domain of darkness" and safely placed "into the kingdom of the Son He loves" (v. 13). Jesus is our Rescuer. What was the result of this rescue mission? "We have redemption," and "forgiveness of sins," Paul proclaimed in verse 14. Jesus' death, burial, and resurrection accomplished this for us.

Paul went on to explain that Jesus is not just our Savior. He is part of the Godhead and was there at Creation. He not only created everything, but He holds it all together, and He chose to give His life to reconcile us to Him. Now that is a compelling reason to praise God!

1 Thessalonians 2:1–12
A Lasting Investment

For you yourselves know, brothers, that our visit with you was not without result. On the contrary, after we had previously suffered, and we were treated outrageously in Philippi, as you know, we were emboldened by our God to speak the gospel of God to you in spite of great opposition. For our exhortation didn't come from error or impurity or an intent to deceive. Instead, just as we have been approved by God to be entrusted with the gospel, so we speak, not to please men, but rather God, who examines our hearts. For we never used flattering speech, as you know, or had greedy motives—God is our witness—and we didn't seek glory from people, either from you or from others. Although we could have been a burden as Christ's apostles, instead we were gentle among you, as a nursing mother nurtures her own children. We cared so much for you that we were pleased to share with you not only the gospel of God but also our own lives, because you had become dear to us. For you remember our labor and hardship, brothers. Working night and day so that we would not burden any of you, we preached God's gospel to you. You are witnesses, and so is God, of how devoutly, righteously, and blamelessly we conducted ourselves with you believers. As you know, like a father

with his own children, we encouraged, comforted,
and implored each one of you to walk worthy of
God, who calls you into His own kingdom and
glory.

Youth development programs in rural areas are amazing opera-
tions to observe. Children invest months into raising livestock
that will be judged at a local fair. They feed and groom the animals,
and many come to love their charges. The animals respond to the care
they receive, and in time they come to know and trust their owners.
In a way, the children's work fine-tuning the lives of these creatures
resembles how parents pour themselves into their children.

Paul expressed similar thoughts regarding how much he and the
apostles with him loved the Christians in Thessalonica and poured into
their lives. He explained how they had tirelessly nourished the church
with the love of Christ, so that they could know Him and continue
to live for Him. The church served as Paul's children, in whom he
invested his life through labors of love.

How are you managing your investments? Whose lives do you
impact? Do you give all you have to those you spiritually feed? What
can you do to be a loving "parent"?

Ask the Lord to strengthen you that you might instill His love in
others. Request His help to reveal himself in all that you do, so that
others can't help but live their lives for Him, and in turn, nurture
others.

John 1:1–14
Full of Grace and Truth

*In the beginning was the Word, and the Word
was with God, and the Word was God. He was
with God in the beginning. All things were created
through Him, and apart from Him not one thing
was created that has been created. Life was in
Him, and that life was the light of men. That light
shines in the darkness, yet the darkness did not
overcome it.*

*There was a man named John who was sent
from God. He came as a witness to testify about
the light, so that all might believe through him. He
was not the light, but he came to testify about the
light. The true light, who gives light to everyone, was
coming into the world.*

*He was in the world, and the world was cre-
ated through Him, yet the world did not recognize
Him. He came to His own, and His own people did
not receive Him. But to all who did receive Him,
He gave them the right to be children of God, to
those who believe in His name, who were born, not
of blood, or of the will of the flesh, or of the will of
man, but of God.*

*The Word became flesh and took up residence
among us. We observed His glory, the glory as the
One and Only Son from the Father, full of grace
and truth.*

When God's people thought about the promised Messiah, they probably would have finished that final sentence differently. Perhaps they would have said "full of power and authority, royalty, and favor" or "full of physical strength, a powerful presence, and the ability to overthrow Rome." But "full of grace and truth"? Nobody would have been expecting that. The Jewish religious leaders sure didn't exhibit much grace, and truth was a word they would rather have defined themselves. They weren't looking for those qualities in themselves, much less in the one who was coming to save them.

Sound familiar? The thing about Jesus is that He came on God's terms and with His agenda, not man's. He didn't come to overturn the human government, but to turn people's ways of thinking about life upside down. He came to save His people from their sins, not from Rome. His destination was not an earthly throne; it was the cross. That changes everything.

Jesus is Truth, even when it offends. He is Truth, even when it's uncomfortable. He is Truth, even when we don't like what truth is. Jesus is also full of grace. He is grace for those who offend. He is grace for those who make us uncomfortable. He is grace for those we don't like.

In Jesus, truth is always covered with grace. If you want to know the fullness of God's glory, embrace both and offer them to others.

2 Thessalonians 1:3–12
The Promise of Relief

We must always thank God for you, broth-
ers. This is right, since your faith is flourishing and
the love each one of you has for one another is
increasing. Therefore, we ourselves boast about
you among God's churches—about your endurance
and faith in all the persecutions and afflictions you
endure. It is a clear evidence of God's righteous
judgment that you will be counted worthy of God's
kingdom, for which you also are suffering, since it
is righteous for God to repay with affliction those
who afflict you and to reward with rest you who
are afflicted, along with us. This will take place at
the revelation of the Lord Jesus from heaven with
His powerful angels, taking vengeance with flaming
fire on those who don't know God and on those
who don't obey the gospel of our Lord Jesus. These
will pay the penalty of eternal destruction from
the Lord's presence and from His glorious strength
in that day when He comes to be glorified by His
saints and to be admired by all those who have
believed, because our testimony among you was
believed. And in view of this, we always pray for
you that our God will consider you worthy of His
calling, and will, by His power, fulfill every desire for
goodness and the work of faith, so that the name
of our Lord Jesus will be glorified by you, and you

*by Him, according to the grace of our God and
the Lord Jesus Christ.*

Researchers have found that rats thrown into water can swim for ten minutes before they drown. However, if they are picked up for just a few seconds every three minutes, they will swim almost indefinitely. If they have just the smallest promise of relief, they can handle so much more than without that promise.

We humans are not that different when it comes to the hope of relief. That is what Paul gives to us here: the promise of strong, just, powerful relief for all of those who have suffered for Christ. Even the words he uses are meant to infuse power into a weak soul. He speaks of "powerful angels" (v. 7), "flaming fire" (v. 8), and "His glorious strength" (v. 9)!

Can you get a mental picture of Jesus leading the charge down from heaven with a flaming sword to bring you rest? Take this mental picture from the Word of God, and remember it when you are weary of doing good, for it is the truth and the promise of help that can sustain you another day. God will not only sustain you but strengthen you to bring Him glory. Ask God to help you remember that He sees you when you suffer, and He will bring you relief in due time.

1 Timothy 5:1–8
Taking Responsibility

Do not rebuke an older man, but exhort him as a father, younger men as brothers, older women as mothers, and with all propriety, the younger women as sisters.

Support widows who are genuinely widows. But if any widow has children or grandchildren, they must learn to practice godliness toward their own family first and to repay their parents, for this pleases God. The real widow, left all alone, has put her hope in God and continues night and day in her petitions and prayers; however, she who is self-indulgent is dead even while she lives. Command this also, so they won't be blamed. But if anyone does not provide for his own, that is his own house-hold, he has denied the faith and is worse than an unbeliever.

Jesus called His followers to be willing to give up the pleasures of family life to follow Him. He does not call us to give up family responsibilities, however. Jesus must come first, but our families are not to be neglected as we serve Him.

In 1 Timothy 5, Paul focused on taking responsibility for our family. Paul said that family members have a duty to care for one another. When Christians fail their family, they live contrary to the teaching of the Bible and are, in this particular situation, worse than an unbeliever.

The Bible tells us that the care of our family is our personal responsibility. We should not relegate the care of our family to the community, government, our friends, or even to other family members who we think have more time than we do. As long as their physical needs do not exceed our capacity for care, we should provide for them. Our families are not only our responsibility but also our blessing.

In America, there is often talk about the burdens of the "sandwich generation." This term refers to mostly middle-aged adults who have the task of caring for both growing children and aging parents. Sadly, it is not uncommon for the middle generation to choose to neglect the care of the older generation due to time or distance. But they can't take all the blame, because the older adults often don't expect their children to provide any care for them in their old age. Neither of these perspectives match the mandate that Paul laid out in the verses above.

In some cultures it is common for multiple generations to live together in the same house, with all members taking responsibility to care for each other. Care is not considered a burden; it's a cultural norm. They don't question it; it's just what they do.

What would happen if younger and older members of families in all societies and cultures cared for each other? What would happen if young and old in the family had a common vision of just who their family should be? What an example to an unbelieving world of how we love each other!

1 Corinthians 13:1–13
Loving People

If I speak human or angelic languages but do not have love, I am a sounding gong or a clanging cymbal. If I have the gift of prophecy and understand all mysteries and all knowledge, and if I have all faith so that I can move mountains but do not have love, I am nothing. And if I donate all my goods to feed the poor, and if I give my body in order to boast but do not have love, I gain nothing. Love is patient, love is kind. Love does not envy, is not boastful, is not conceited, does not act improperly, is not selfish, is not provoked, and does not keep a record of wrongs. Love finds no joy in unrighteousness but rejoices in the truth. It bears all things, believes all things, hopes all things, endures all things.

Love never ends. But as for prophecies, they will come to an end; as for languages, they will cease; as for knowledge, it will come to an end. For we know in part, and we prophesy in part. But when the perfect comes, the partial will come to an end. When I was a child, I spoke like a child, I thought like a child, I reasoned like a child. When I became a man, I put aside childish things. For now we see indistinctly, as in a mirror, but then face to face. Now I know in part, but then I will know fully, as I am fully known. Now these three remain: faith, hope, and love. But the greatest of these is love.

Many people refer to 1 Corinthians 13 as the love chapter. Brides and grooms use it in their wedding ceremonies. Popular Valentine cards use its words for inspiration. However, the passage is about more than romantic love. The love Paul spoke of is God's kind of love, an unconditional love that can endure any circumstance.

Loving people love people. Those who have love inside can demonstrate love toward others. If love is not present in you, you can't give it to others. But if you have trusted in Christ and have the love of God in your heart, you can love others even in difficult circumstances.

Paul told the Corinthians that love could bear all things. Love caused people to believe even in the most challenging circumstances. Love produces hope and endures many hardships. Love never ends (v. 8).

Since "God is love" (1 John 4:16), the only way to know love is to know God. When you come to know God, His love is poured into your heart through the Holy Spirit, making you a loving person (see Rom. 5:5). As a loving person, you are able to love people, no matter who they are or what they might have done to you.

2 Timothy 1:8–14
Confidence in Christ

So don't be ashamed of the testimony about our Lord, or of me His prisoner. Instead, share in suffering for the gospel, relying on the power of God.

He has saved us and called us with a holy calling, not according to our works, but according to His own purpose and grace, which was given to us in Christ Jesus before time began. This has now been made evident through the appearing of our Savior Christ Jesus, who has abolished death and has brought life and immortality to light through the gospel.

For this gospel I was appointed a herald, apostle, and teacher, and that is why I suffer these things. But I am not ashamed, because I know the One I have believed in and am persuaded that He is able to guard what has been entrusted to me until that day.

Hold on to the pattern of sound teaching that you have heard from me, in the faith and love that are in Christ Jesus. Guard, through the Holy Spirit who lives in us, that good thing entrusted to you.

We've all known those people who seem constantly self-sufficient and confident. Nothing seems to shake their ability to handle themselves with ease and grace. It might be the star performer at work who, by all appearances, glides through the day with effortless ease. Perhaps it's the mom-of-four who always looks put together, whose children are well behaved, and who manages to volunteer at three ministries—all with a smile on her face. Or maybe it's the college student who knows exactly what he wants to do with his life, is in a stable relationship with a great young woman, and almost inexplicably likes to spend time with your crazy family on the weekend. We know these people must have problems and obstacles in their lives, yet they manage to keep pressing on with joy and confidence. How do they do it?

The apostle Paul probably had a large helping of confidence, though his life experiences certainly could have shaken his grit. In his writing to Timothy, Paul emphasized that even though he had suffered imprisonment and abuse, nothing could impact his confidence in Christ. God has entrusted His people with that confidence. Paul's message is that while man may abandon and abuse us, no one can take from us God's gracious gift of salvation.

Life is full of ups and downs. Yet, even if we struggle with insecurities and decreased confidence in ourselves, we can still live convinced and assured of God's love. If you need renewed confidence in God right now, say this prayer: "Father, remind me of my worth. Help me to remember the price You paid for my salvation and confidently let others see what You have done in my life."

Luke 10:1–12, 17–20
The Harvest

After this, the Lord appointed 70 others, and He sent them ahead of Him in pairs to every town and place where He Himself was about to go. He told them: "The harvest is abundant, but the workers are few. Therefore, pray to the Lord of the harvest to send out workers into His harvest. Now go; I'm sending you out like lambs among wolves. Don't carry a money-bag, traveling bag, or sandals; don't greet anyone along the road. Whatever house you enter, first say, 'Peace to this household.' If a son of peace is there, your peace will rest on him; but if not, it will return to you. Remain in the same house, eating and drinking what they offer, for the worker is worthy of his wages. Don't be moving from house to house. When you enter any town, and they welcome you, eat the things set before you. Heal the sick who are there, and tell them, 'The kingdom of God has come near you.' When you enter any town, and they don't welcome you, go out into its streets and say,' We are wiping off as a witness against you even the dust of your town that clings to our feet. Know this for certain: The kingdom of God has come near.' I tell you, on that day it will be more tolerable for Sodom than for that town. . . .

The Seventy returned with joy, saying, "Lord, even the demons submit to us in Your name."

He said to them, "I watched Satan fall from heaven like a lightning flash. Look, I have given you the authority to trample on snakes and scorpions and over all the power of the enemy; nothing will ever harm you. However, don't rejoice that the spirits submit to you, but rejoice that your names are written in heaven."

Here we encounter one of the favorite verses of mission-sending agencies: "The harvest is abundant, but the workers are few. Therefore, pray to the Lord of the harvest to send out workers into His harvest" (v. 2).

But we rarely hear what comes next: "I'm sending you out like lambs among wolves." Whoa! That doesn't sound so great. Or fun. Or *safe*. But send out His men Jesus did. And it was an urgent task. He gave them many instructions about what they should or shouldn't do: Don't take anything extra with you. Don't waste time with long greetings (that were typical in that day, but not required if someone was in a hurry). If people welcome you, that's great; serve them and tell them the kingdom of God is near. If they don't, move along.

We know that their work was successful, for they returned to Jesus with joy and awe at what they had been given the power to do. But even so, Jesus told them their joy should not be based on that power, but on the fact that they would spend eternity with Him in heaven.

We would do well to follow in these men's footsteps. Yes, we will face opposition in this world, but we must be urgent about sharing the good news of Jesus. In the end our reward will be great—eternal life!

Titus 3:1–11

Be Ready for Every Good Work

*Remind them to be submissive to rulers and author-
ities, to obey, to be ready for every good work,
to slander no one, to avoid fighting, and to be
kind, always showing gentleness to all people. For
we too were once foolish, disobedient, deceived,
enslaved by various passions and pleasures, living
in malice and envy, hateful, detesting one another.*

*But when the goodness of God and His love
for mankind appeared, He saved us—not by works
of righteousness that we had done, but according
to His mercy, through the washing of regeneration
and renewal by the Holy Spirit. He poured out this
Spirit on us abundantly through Jesus Christ our
Savior, so that having been justified by His grace,
we may become heirs with the hope of eternal life.*

*This saying is trustworthy. I want you to insist on
these things, so that those who have believed God
might be careful to devote themselves to good
works. These are good and profitable for everyone.
But avoid foolish debates, genealogies, quarrels,
and disputes about the law, for they are unprofit-
able and worthless. Reject a divisive person after
a first and second warning, knowing that such a
person is perverted and sins, being self-condemned.*

Week after week the ladies would gather together for morning coffee. These were good women, servants at the church, faithful to assist with church needs. But the ladies' gathering shifted from the eternal to the temporal. What started as a few moms from the church praying and having coffee turned into a session of gossip and character assassination. The longer they met together, the more their conversation turned to negative talk, and they neglected to pray and encourage each other. Instead, they were quick to judge sin in others and ignore their own.

Paul, in Titus, continued to develop the church through his discipleship of Titus. In chapter 3, he encouraged Titus to be subject to authorities in his life that would spur him on and lead to good. He reminded Titus not to get caught up in his old ways of disobedience, not to be trapped with the sin that once was so enslaving.

One by one, members of the ladies group died, but along the way, friendships were broken, children walked away from the church, and marriages failed. Then, starting with one changed heart, several of the ladies reached out to the Lord, and the things that had been foolish faded away because of His mercy and love. The women began to pray again, to study the Scriptures, and to do "good works."

Do you find yourself straying from the truth and participating in sinful and foolish talk and actions? If not, ask God to help you stay strong. If so, ask Him to have mercy on you and change your heart. Ask Him to help you "be ready for every good work" and walk away from things that are not of Him.

2 Timothy 3:10–17
The Purpose of Scripture

But you have followed my teaching, conduct, purpose, faith, patience, love, and endurance, along with the persecutions and sufferings that came to me in Antioch, Iconium, and Lystra. What persecutions I endured! Yet the Lord rescued me from them all. In fact, all those who want to live a godly life in Christ Jesus will be persecuted. Evil people and impostors will become worse, deceiving and being deceived. But as for you, continue in what you have learned and firmly believed. You know those who taught you, and you know that from childhood you have known the sacred Scriptures, which are able to give you wisdom for salvation through faith in Christ Jesus. All Scripture is inspired by God and is profitable for teaching, for rebuking, for correcting, for training in righteousness, so that the man of God may be complete, equipped for every good work.

A person's last words are often the most important, and in this last letter to his disciple Timothy, Paul was adamant about the purpose and value of God's Word. Paul never wasted time or influence. Obviously he valued the Scriptures highly (2 Tim. 4:13).

The Bible was written by men who were divinely inspired. By His Spirit, God breathed His holy breath upon the human authors, who penned the precise words He desired. He did not override their personalities or wills but worked through them to produce the Word from God that is without error; thus, it is totally true and trustworthy.

Christians who study the Bible and apply what they learn will grow in holiness and avoid many pitfalls in this world. The Old Testament Scriptures point to Christ, revealing the depth of our sin and our need for a Savior. The Gospels reveal Christ as that Savior, and much of the remaining New Testament instructs us how to live out our faith in Him.

Bible study is critical for a Christian to grow in his faith in Christ. Period. Many godly men and women have written Bible studies that have helped millions of people draw near to the Father. Bible studies, though, are not Scripture. They are based on Scripture and can be beneficial to Christian growth, but they aren't the Bible. There is no substitute for opening your copy of God's Word and asking Him to speak to you through His own words.

A good study Bible can be helpful in defining words, showing maps, and explaining cultural references and such that you will come across in your reading. It can help you understand Scripture more clearly and know how to apply its message to life. Make no mistake— other books and studies are good, but there is no substitute for the Bible.

Philemon 8–21
Siblings in Christ

For this reason, although I have great boldness in Christ to command you to do what is right, I appeal to you, instead, on the basis of love. I, Paul, as an elderly man and now also as a prisoner of Christ Jesus, appeal to you for my son, Onesimus. I fathered him while I was in chains. Once he was useless to you, but now he is useful both to you and to me. I am sending him back to you as a part of myself. I wanted to keep him with me, so that in my imprisonment for the gospel he might serve me in your place. But I didn't want to do anything without your consent, so that your good deed might not be out of obligation, but of your own free will. For perhaps this is why he was sepa-rated from you for a brief time, so that you might get him back permanently, no longer as a slave, but more than a slave—as a dearly loved brother. He is especially so to me, but even more to you, both in the flesh and in the Lord.

So if you consider me a partner, accept him as you would me. And if he has wronged you in any way, or owes you anything, charge that to my account. I, Paul, write this with my own hand: I will repay it—not to mention to you that you owe me even your own self. Yes, brother, may I have joy from you in the Lord; refresh my heart in Christ.

Since I am confident of your obedience, I am writing to you, knowing that you will do even more than I say.

We all seem to know how brothers should not behave. We have seen brothers (and sisters) arguing and fighting in lines at the grocery store, at family reunions, in playgrounds, and in countless other situations. It typically makes everyone around them uncomfortable, especially when they are adults. We know how siblings are supposed to act. We are to show unconditional love and acceptance to those who are our brothers and sisters, whether through blood or though faith.

Paul, who was in prison when he wrote this short letter, had led a slave named Onesimus to faith in Jesus Christ. He called this slave a "dearly loved" brother, a Greek word indicating the highest form of love. If Paul, a prisoner in a Roman cell, could call a slave who was a fellow believer a brother, how can we do less? Paul called himself a partner with Philemon (Onesiumus's owner, who had once found Onesimus "useless") and asked the slave owner to receive the slave as his brother—showing a type of love for this man that transcends what the world knows.

We don't deserve the forgiveness God gives us, but our acceptance of Jesus' sacrifice gives us the opportunity to call all believers "brothers." If you don't already think of and treat other Christians as your brothers and sisters, ask God to change your heart and actions.

Hebrews 2:1–9
Where Were You?

We must, therefore, pay even more attention to what we have heard, so that we will not drift away. For if the message spoken through angels was legally binding and every transgression and disobedience received a just punishment, how will we escape if we neglect such a great salvation? It was first spoken by the Lord and was confirmed to us by those who heard Him. At the same time, God also testified by signs and wonders, various miracles, and distributions of gifts from the Holy Spirit according to His will.

For He has not subjected to angels the world to come that we are talking about. But one has somewhere testified: What is man that You remember him, or the son of man that You care for him? You made him lower than the angels for a short time; You crowned him with glory and honor and subjected everything under his feet.

For in subjecting everything to him, He left nothing that is not subject to him. As it is, we do not yet see everything subjected to him. But we do see Jesus—made lower than the angels for a short time so that by God's grace He might taste death for everyone—crowned with glory and honor because of His suffering in death.

When a major historical event occurs, most people can remember exactly where they were when it happened. Boomers can give you a detailed description of the day President John F. Kennedy was assassinated and the day man first walked on the moon. Generation Xers know precisely what they were doing when the space shuttle *Challenger* exploded in the sky just after takeoff. Both of those groups, as well as those even younger, can vividly remember watching the Twin Towers fall in New York City on September 11, 2001.

Oftentimes as the days pass, these events that were so important to us seem to slip back into the recesses of our minds, seldom pondered. Yet the mere mention of a name or a date can bring those memories right back as if they happened just yesterday.

But those events are mere blips on the radar of history compared to the greatest event ever. The good news of Jesus Christ is the most important news that has ever been delivered or will be delivered. Those of us who have become believers can remember the first time we heard the gospel or, if we grew up hearing the good news, we can tell you exactly when and how we came to a saving faith. In the book of Hebrews, the author tells us that this great news must not slip to the back of our minds.

We are told to pay attention to the gospel of Christ, so we do not drift from Him. There is a link between heeding what we have heard and drifting. The more earnestly we seek Christ, the closer we remain to Him. The farther away the gospel is in our minds, the farther Christ is as well. Thus, we must cling to the anchor of Christ, remembering what He has done, so He will be at the forefront of our minds and lives. We must give heed to the gospel.

—Day 69—

1 Corinthians 1:10–15
Keep It Together

Now I urge you, brothers, in the name of our Lord Jesus Christ, that all of you agree in what you say, that there be no divisions among you, and that you be united with the same understanding and the same conviction. For it has been reported to me about you, my brothers, by members of Chloe's household, that there is rivalry among you. What I am saying is this: Each of you says, "I'm with Paul," or "I'm with Apollos," or "I'm with Cephas," or "I'm with Christ." Is Christ divided? Was it Paul who was crucified for you? Or were you baptized in Paul's name? I thank God that I baptized none of you except Crispus and Gaius, so that no one can say you were baptized in my name.

Picture a pair of sneakers on your feet. As you prepare for a quick walk, you notice your shoes aren't facing the same way. One foot is facing forward, while the other is facing backward. With every step, your feet will pull you in opposite directions. How far could you walk before you fall?

Though this scenario is silly (as well as physically impossible), it represents what happened in the Corinthian church. Worn down by the fatigue of immaturity and spiritual warfare, church members lost their unified focus on advancing Christ's kingdom. They began to form factions and perhaps argued with each other about petty issues and ministry agendas. Sad to say, the same thing happens today.

We bicker about things like worship style, paint color, and whether we should have pews or chairs. We argue about whether we should give money to people who can't pay their bills—are we being generous or are we enabling them; should we counsel them instead? Then there's the debate about Sunday school versus small groups (or discipleship groups or missional communities). Which is best? When should they meet? The arguments are endless, and they can tear a church apart. Paul tells us we need to be united. Do we have to agree on every tiny detail of church life? No. But we do need to be united in our mission and our commission to share the gospel.

We need to be united in who we follow. We could easily replace Paul, Apollos, or Cephas in the verses above with John Calvin, Francis Schaeffer, or Tim Keller, and they would be accurate for today's church. All too often we focus on earthly leaders, and to do so is dangerous. We need to set aside these divisions among us and remember who we really follow—Christ. He was the one who was crucified for us. We were baptized in His name.

If the body of Christ isn't positioned to go the same direction, saying the same thing about our Lord and His priorities, we can't move forward to fulfill the Great Commission. Jesus is the one we follow, and we must unite behind Him and His teachings.

Hebrews 6:10–20
God Cannot Lie

*For God is not unjust; He will not forget your work
and the love you showed for His name when
you served the saints—and you continue to serve
them. Now we want each of you to demonstrate
the same diligence for the final realization of your
hope, so that you won't become lazy but will be
imitators of those who inherit the promises through
faith and perseverance.*

*For when God made a promise to Abraham,
since He had no one greater to swear by, He swore
by Himself: I will indeed bless you, and I will greatly
multiply you.*

*And so, after waiting patiently, Abraham
obtained the promise. For men swear by something
greater than themselves, and for them a confirming
oath ends every dispute. Because God wanted to
show His unchangeable purpose even more clearly
to the heirs of the promise, He guaranteed it with
an oath, so that through two unchangeable things,
in which it is impossible for God to lie, we who
have fled for refuge might have strong encouragement to seize the hope set before us. We have this
hope as an anchor for our lives, safe and secure. It
enters the inner sanctuary behind the curtain. Jesus
has entered there on our behalf as a forerunner,*

because He has become a high priest forever in the order of Melchizedek.

W e've seen the following scene countless time in movies, on television, and perhaps even live in a courtroom: A witness places his or her hand on a Bible and swears to tell the truth, the whole truth, and nothing but the truth.

This practice symbolizes mankind's effort to find the truth of a matter in a court of law. We often find the truth elusive, but God has no such problem. The Bible reveals that for God, it's impossible to lie.

When a man takes an oath to tell the truth, he must swear by that which is greater than he—something unquestionable. When God takes an oath, there is no greater thing on which to swear than on Himself. His truthfulness is guaranteed by two unchangeable realities: who He is and what He has said.

When God promises something, we can know He means it just by virtue of who He is. The Word of God overflows with the promises of God. He made promises to men like Abraham, Moses, David, and the disciples. He also makes promises to us through His Word. We can be sure He will follow through on those promises.

Hebrews 10:1–14
Sacrifice

Since the law has only a shadow of the good things to come, and not the actual form of those realities, it can never perfect the worshipers by the same sacrifices they continually offer year after year. Otherwise, wouldn't they have stopped being offered, since the worshipers, once purified, would no longer have any consciousness of sins? But in the sacrifices there is a reminder of sins every year. For it is impossible for the blood of bulls and goats to take away sins.

Therefore, as He was coming into the world, He said:

You did not want sacrifice and offering, but You prepared a body for Me. You did not delight in whole burnt offerings and sin offerings. Then I said, "See—it is written about Me in the volume of the scroll—I have come to do Your will, God!"

After He says above, You did not want or delight in sacrifices and offerings, whole burnt offerings and sin offerings (which are offered according to the law), He then says, See, I have come to do Your will. He takes away the first to establish the second. By this will of God, we have been sanctified through the offering of the body of Jesus Christ once and for all.

*Every priest stands day after day ministering
and offering the same sacrifices time after time,
which can never take away sins. But this man, after
offering one sacrifice for sins forever, sat down at
the right hand of God. He is now waiting until His
enemies are made His footstool. For by one offering
He has perfected forever those who are sanctified.*

The Jewish sacrificial system called for regular sacrifices and offerings to be made to atone for sin. The writer of Hebrews declared that those sacrifices were no longer necessary to be reconciled with God. Through the death of Christ, the sacrificial requirement had been met once and for all.

In biblical times, priests would stand in the holy place (at first in the tabernacle and later in the temple) and perform the rituals God required for forgiveness. However, those sacrifices only brought temporary purification. They could not take away sins.

Christ came to do God's will. When Jesus offered His body on the cross, He made the final sacrifice—the only acceptable payment for humanity's sins. Note that the writer contrasted the priests' standing while making the sacrifice, but Christ sat down at the right hand of God. This is a clear indication that His sacrifice was sufficient and that God's requirement was met. He did it all for all!

To receive the free gift of salvation, we must repent of our sins and confess our faith in Jesus, the one who sacrificed His life for us.

Ephesians 2:1–10
Dead in Sins, Alive in Christ

And you were dead in your trespasses and sins in which you previously walked according to the ways of this world, according to the ruler who exercises authority over the lower heavens, the spirit now working in the disobedient. We too all previously lived among them in our fleshly desires, carrying out the inclinations of our flesh and thoughts, and we were by nature children under wrath as the others were also. But God, who is rich in mercy, because of His great love that He had for us, made us alive with the Messiah even though we were dead in trespasses. You are saved by grace! Together with Christ Jesus He also raised us up and seated us in the heavens, so that in the coming ages He might display the immeasurable riches of His grace through His kindness to us in Christ Jesus. For you are saved by grace through faith, and this is not from yourselves; it is God's gift—not from works, so that no one can boast. For we are His creation, created in Christ Jesus for good works, which God prepared ahead of time so that we should walk in them.

Lewis Carroll's Alice, from *Alice's Adventures in Wonderland*, once asked for directions from the Cheshire Cat. "Would you tell me, please, which way I ought to go from here?" The Cat responded, "That depends a good deal on where you want to get to." "I don't much care where," said Alice. "Then it doesn't matter which way you go," said the Cat.

In our lives, it *does* matter which way we go. We can choose the path of sin and death, or we can choose life in Christ. Our default position is a life of sin. We can tool along on cruise control through that life forever unless we choose to change course.

Paul says that sinful people who deserve nothing but God's wrath can be redeemed by His grace. Is your life cut off from God and controlled by your own selfish desires? The world tells us not to take responsibility for our sins. We can blame anything and everything in life on circumstances, but we really have no one to blame but ourselves. We choose to sin, but by God's grace, we can be saved.

God gives us a choice. If you have not yet chosen to follow Christ, now is the time to decide which way to go. The choice for you is not fiction, however. You have the responsibility to choose which way you will go, and the consequences are eternal. God is always the right choice. It is by His grace you are saved, to eternal and abundant life.

Hebrews 11:1–10
Little Guys, Big God

Now faith is the reality of what is hoped for, the proof of what is not seen. For our ancestors won God's approval by it.

By faith we understand that the universe was created by God's command, so that what is seen has been made from things that are not visible.

By faith Abel offered to God a better sacrifice than Cain did. By faith he was approved as a righteous man, because God approved his gifts, and even though he is dead, he still speaks through his faith.

By faith Enoch was taken away so he did not experience death, and he was not to be found because God took him away. For prior to his removal he was approved, since he had pleased God. Now without faith it is impossible to please God, for the one who draws near to Him must believe that He exists and rewards those who seek Him.

By faith Noah, after he was warned about what was not yet seen and motivated by godly fear, built an ark to deliver his family. By faith he condemned the world and became an heir of the righteousness that comes by faith.

By faith Abraham, when he was called, obeyed and went out to a place he was going to receive as an inheritance. He went out, not knowing where he was going. By faith he stayed as a foreigner in the land of promise, living in tents with Isaac and Jacob, coheirs of the same promise. For he was looking forward to the city that has foundations, whose architect and builder is God.

E very Hall of Fame is made up of ordinary people who do extraordinary things. In the Country Music Hall of Fame, you find people like Loretta Lynn, the coal miner's daughter, who started life as an ordinary person but achieved stardom through her music. In the Baseball Hall of Fame in Cooperstown, you discover Hank Aaron came from humble beginnings in Mobile, Alabama, but he achieved stardom by eclipsing the great Babe Ruth's record for the most home runs in a career.

Some see Hebrews 11 as a Hall of Fame of faith. Really it is a list of ordinary people—with an all-powerful God. Abel offered a better sacrifice to God than Cain, and God still is using Abel's story to encourage others (v. 4). Enoch walked with God, and God spared him from death (v. 5). The writer commended Noah for building a boat but highlighted God for warning him (v. 7). He noted that Abraham left his homeland but God provided a place even better than the Promised Land (vv. 8–10).

Are you small in stature or in faith? The writer of Hebrews emphasized that no matter how big or small, people need faith to please God, and He will reward those who seek Him.

1 Corinthians 15:12–22
Affirmation of Resurrection

Now if Christ is proclaimed as raised from the dead, how can some of you say, "There is no resurrection of the dead"? But if there is no resurrection of the dead, then Christ has not been raised; and if Christ has not been raised, then our proclamation is without foundation, and so is your faith. In addition, we are found to be false witnesses about God, because we have testified about God that He raised up Christ—whom He did not raise up if in fact the dead are not raised. For if the dead are not raised, Christ has not been raised. And if Christ has not been raised, your faith is worthless; you are still in your sins. Therefore, those who have fallen asleep in Christ have also perished. If we have put our hope in Christ for this life only, we should be pitied more than anyone.

But now Christ has been raised from the dead, the firstfruits of those who have fallen asleep. For since death came through a man, the resurrection of the dead also comes through a man. For as in Adam all die, so also in Christ all will be made alive.

As with any good sermon, our investigation of the resurrection of Jesus includes "what" (the facts) and "so what" (the significance of the facts). In Paul's day, some were saying that there was no resurrection of the dead. This belief was a huge problem, because resurrection from the dead is a central tenet of the Christian faith. Paul explained that if Jesus didn't rise from the dead, then His followers don't have a leg to stand on, because our testimony is dependent upon God raising Christ from the dead. If Christ is still dead, we are also still dead in our sins. We have no reason for our faith.

The resurrection of Jesus Christ means many things to many people, but particularly to the redeemed. Jesus' resurrection confirms His identity, gives heaven's seal of approval on all He taught and promised, and blasts a path through the grave for you and me to be raised.

In the early 1940s, during the Nazi occupation of France, the Germans sealed the border to stop citizens from fleeing. However, one small town sitting atop the border was found to be losing population at a swift pace. Locals had remembered that the ancient cemetery had a gate in the rear, closed for over a century. They reopened it. From then on, when attending funerals, the citizens entered from the front, but kept right on walking through the graveyard into the land of the free.

When Jesus rose from the dead, He opened a gate in the back of the cemetery. We still go there, but we don't stay. We walk out the back door into the land of eternal freedom.

James 2:1–13
Do Not Show Favoritism

My brothers, do not show favoritism as you hold on to the faith in our glorious Lord Jesus Christ. For example, a man comes into your meeting wearing a gold ring and dressed in fine clothes, and a poor man dressed in dirty clothes also comes in. If you look with favor on the man wearing the fine clothes and say, "Sit here in a good place," and yet you say to the poor man, "Stand over there," or, "Sit here on the floor by my footstool," haven't you discriminated among yourselves and become judges with evil thoughts?

Listen, my dear brothers: Didn't God choose the poor in this world to be rich in faith and heirs of the kingdom that He has promised to those who love Him? Yet you dishonored that poor man. Don't the rich oppress you and drag you into the courts? Don't they blaspheme the noble name that was pronounced over you at your baptism?

Indeed, if you keep the royal law prescribed in the Scripture, Love your neighbor as yourself, you are doing well. But if you show favoritism, you commit sin and are convicted by the law as transgressors. For whoever keeps the entire law, yet fails in one point, is guilty of breaking it all. For He who said, Do not commit adultery, also said, Do not murder. So if you do not commit adultery, but you do murder, you are a lawbreaker.

Speak and act as those who will be judged by the law of freedom. For judgment is without mercy to the one who hasn't shown mercy. Mercy triumphs over judgment.

A few years ago, a new pastor disguised himself as a homeless man. He lived outside, without food or shelter, for an entire week. On Sunday, he entered the church building still dirty and unshaven. Many people ignored him or shunned him. But there were a few who actually demonstrated love and concern. Once the pastor revealed his identity, he stressed the fact that everyone deserves a gentle word and acts of kindness. Even those who appear to be unlovely are still worthy of genuine care.

Why would someone who is unkempt, lazy, or unwise deserve loving-kindness? Why should we be compassionate, even toward those who have broken the law? Why should we not show favor to Christians over those of other faiths? Because we are all made in the image of God. Deep inside, we're all the same, with identical needs. And as creations of God, we all have value. All are deserving of our love, of our service, and of hearing the good news of Jesus.

As you pass others today, try to see them through God's eyes. Remember that the homeless woman, the Muslim family, the chronically unemployed man, the woman on the street corner are all fellow sinners in need of grace. Let your words and actions be a reflection of the Lord's love. Ask God to help you see all people as valuable in His eyes and treat them with love and respect.

Revelation 21:1–7
What a Difference He Makes

*Then I saw a new heaven and a new earth, for the
first heaven and the first earth had passed away,
and the sea no longer existed. I also saw the Holy
City, new Jerusalem, coming down out of heaven
from God, prepared like a bride adorned for her
husband.*

*Then I heard a loud voice from the throne:
Look! God's dwelling is with humanity, and He will
live with them. They will be His people, and God
Himself will be with them and be their God. He will
wipe away every tear from their eyes. Death will no
longer exist; grief, crying, and pain will exist no longer, because the previous things have passed away.*

*Then the One seated on the throne said, "Look!
I am making everything new." He also said, "Write,
because these words are faithful and true." And
He said to me, "It is done! I am the Alpha and
the Omega, the Beginning and the End. I will give
water as a gift to the thirsty from the spring of life.
The victor will inherit these things, and I will be his
God, and he will be My son.*

The apostle John saw his and all believers' future with God, heard
a voice explaining it, and found that mere words were inadequate
to describe it. Painting word pictures of a bride, God's tabernacle,

dwelling and belonging, John tried to help us experience what heaven will be like.

Suddenly, John switches from the grandeur of heaven to addressing the human condition of suffering and how that will change for those with eternal life. And, oh, what a change it is!

A girl became ill at the age of 15, and though she had a myriad of doctors, hospitals, clinics, wonder drugs, treatments, and prayers from her parents, siblings, and a host of other believers, she never got well. After living in almost constant pain for twenty-one years, she went to see and hear for herself what heaven is like. No more tears, no sorrow, no crying, and no more pain are her reality now. What a joy that must be for her!

That will be the reality for all of us who have trusted in Jesus for salvation and have been given the gift of eternal life. What hope that gives us as we travel through this world of pain, suffering, and death— knowing that someday we will be in a place where all of that is taken away and will be replaced with never-ending joy in the presence of our Creator and Savior.

Romans 6:15–23
The Greatest Gift

What then? Should we sin because we are not under law but under grace? Absolutely not! Don't you know that if you offer yourselves to someone as obedient slaves, you are slaves of that one you obey—either of sin leading to death or of obedience leading to righteousness? But thank God that, although you used to be slaves of sin, you obeyed from the heart that pattern of teaching you were transferred to, and having been liberated from sin, you became enslaved to righteousness. I am using a human analogy because of the weakness of your flesh. For just as you offered the parts of yourselves as slaves to moral impurity, and to greater and greater lawlessness, so now offer them as slaves to righteousness, which results in sanctification. For when you were slaves of sin, you were free from allegiance to righteousness. So what fruit was produced then from the things you are now ashamed of? For the end of those things is death. But now, since you have been liberated from sin and have become enslaved to God, you have your fruit, which results in sanctification—and the end is eternal life! For the wages of sin is death, but the gift of God is eternal life in Christ Jesus our Lord.

A group of volunteers boarded a bus in a remote Asian mountain village after telling the story of Jesus in a one-room school, wondering if anyone understood. Just before departure, a young girl came running toward the bus with a red envelope. She stepped onto the bus, gave it to the translator, and asked her to say, "When you get home, please give this to Jesus and thank Him for what He did." Inside was a cheap, plastic necklace, her most treasured possession. She was giving it not as payment for Jesus' work on the cross, but as her way of saying thank you to Him.

Gift-giving is universal. We probably still experience a child-like thrill anytime someone gives us a gift simply because they love us. It cost us nothing, it now belongs to us, and it says someone cares. We didn't do anything to deserve it; it's not payment for something, or it wouldn't technically be a gift. A true gift is given freely and without compulsion. It is given out of love and affection, and at some cost to the giver.

The greatest gift was given out of the deepest, purest love possible. It cost us nothing, but it is not without cost to the giver. This gift of new life, eternal life, was given through the gracious sacrifice of Jesus on the cross. It is given but must be received to be ours. We receive it by turning to God through faith in Jesus Christ.

Galatians 3:1–14
Justified by Faith

You foolish Galatians! Who has hypnotized you, before whose eyes Jesus Christ was vividly por-trayed as crucified? I only want to learn this from you: Did you receive the Spirit by the works of the law or by hearing with faith? Are you so foolish? After beginning with the Spirit, are you now going to be made complete by the flesh? Did you suffer so much for nothing—if in fact it was for nothing? So then, does God supply you with the Spirit and work miracles among you by the works of the law or by hearing with faith?

Just as Abraham believed God, and it was credited to him for righteousness, then understand that those who have faith are Abraham's sons. Now the Scripture saw in advance that God would justify the Gentiles by faith and told the good news ahead of time to Abraham, saying, All the nations will be blessed through you. So those who have faith are blessed with Abraham, who had faith.

For all who rely on the works of the law are under a curse, because it is written: Everyone who does not continue doing everything written in the book of the law is cursed. Now it is clear that no one is justified before God by the law, because the righteous will live by faith. But the law is not based on faith; instead, the one who does these things will live by them. Christ has redeemed us from the curse of the law by becoming a curse for us, because it is written: Everyone who is hung on a tree is cursed. The purpose was that the blessing of Abraham would come to the Gentiles by Christ Jesus, so that we could receive the promised Spirit through faith.

The Galatian churches were struggling against a fierce spiritual attack, and they were tempted to go back to a system of works-based salvation. Paul confronted them with strong words, warning them of the danger of returning to that which could neither save nor enhance their growth as Christians. He reminded them of the truth they had initially received and called them back to faith in Jesus alone.

Many people draw near to the Lord but hesitate to make a faith commitment, thinking they must clean up their lives first. Of course, that's impossible! No one can clean up his life by himself. Only the Lord can do that. Otherwise, works of the law would be sufficient.

Likewise, many Christians think it's up to them to be holy. They begin in faith but continue by works. We can't work our way to holiness any more than we can work our way to salvation. Both are God's gift to us through His Holy Spirit, whom we receive by faith.

James 4:13-17
Tomorrow Is a Mystery

*Come now, you who say, "Today or tomorrow we
will travel to such and such a city and spend a
year there and do business and make a profit."
You don't even know what tomorrow will bring—
what your life will be! For you are like smoke that
appears for a little while, then vanishes.*

*Instead, you should say, "If the Lord wills, we
will live and do this or that." But as it is, you boast
in your arrogance. All such boasting is evil. So it is
a sin for the person who knows to do what is good
and doesn't do it.*

It starts when we're young. We dream about being ballerinas or fire-
men and then, just like that, we reach the point where we can't wait
until that magical age called "teenager." But thirteen is a whole lot like
twelve, so we start looking forward to the freedom of age sixteen. The
novelty of driving wears off quickly though, and we start thinking
about how great life will be when we graduate.

After that, things like landing our ideal job, getting married,
and having kids become our focus. Then we can't wait to retire. It
never stops. There's always something ahead that threatens to steal
our focus—even if it's just looking forward to the weekend. Left
unchecked, those things have the power to prevent us from doing anything meaningful today.

On the other hand, sometimes when we focus on the future, it's not about the good things we want to happen, but it's on the bad things we fear might happen—and we all know from experience that many of those things will never come to pass. We waste so much time thinking about something terrible that might happen that we miss out on the good things happening right now.

It's not bad to look forward to things, have a plan for the future, or take logical measures to mitigate future disasters, but life is short. It is not part of God's plan to waste any moment, day, week, or stage of your life. It is not His plan for you to focus on tomorrow, because, truthfully, tomorrow is a mystery. You don't know what tomorrow will bring.

When we don't focus on today, we might miss something that is important—someone in our presence who needs encouragement or support right now, a seemingly small task that needs to be done in order for there to be a *better* tomorrow, a few moments with a child who may remember that interaction forever. There is so much we can do and focus on in the here and now that there's no reason to hone in on what might or might not happen tomorrow, next week, or in 10 years.

Whether you're looking forward to something or dreading it, the lesson is the same: God never intends for the focus on tomorrow to be your focus today.

Matthew 15:32–38
True Compassion

Now Jesus summoned His disciples and said, "I have compassion on the crowd, because they've already stayed with Me three days and have nothing to eat. I don't want to send them away hungry; otherwise they might collapse on the way."

The disciples said to Him, "Where could we get enough bread in this desolate place to fill such a crowd?"

"How many loaves do you have?" Jesus asked them.

"Seven," they said, "and a few small fish."

After commanding the crowd to sit down on the ground, He took the seven loaves and the fish, and He gave thanks, broke them, and kept on giving them to the disciples, and the disciples gave them to the crowds. They all ate and were filled. Then they collected the leftover pieces—seven large baskets full. Now those who ate were 4,000 men, besides women and children.

Jesus healed the sick, gave sight to the blind, and made the lame walk. The people were amazed and gave glory to God. Jesus also took the opportunity to gather His disciples and teach them a few lessons. First, He taught them to see the crowds through His eyes. Even though they were not asking for food, Jesus was aware of their hunger and had an overwhelming desire to give them something to eat. He didn't just empathize with their situation; Jesus took action.

Sometimes we get so caught up in doing the Lord's work that we miss even the most basic needs of those around us. Compassion is not merely observing the needs of others; it's always accompanied by a desire to ease their suffering.

President Teddy Roosevelt once said, "People don't care how much you know until they know how much you care." That quote is sometimes used in the context of sharing the gospel. The idea is that if we fill someone's physical needs—show that we care—then we have earned the right to tell them about Jesus—what we know. The justification for this method of evangelizing is that Jesus often took care of people's physical needs before he addressed their spiritual needs.

That might sound like a great method on the surface, but when you really think about it, it's a little manipulative. Jesus never told us to have compassion on someone so that we can then tell them about Him. He just wants us to have compassion, period. If that interaction eventually leads to a situation where we have the opportunity to witness to someone, that's great! But we should be driven by compassion, not by other motives.

Developing godly compassion is important and takes daily practice. If often starts with simply taking our eyes off of ourselves and opening our eyes to the people we encounter. There are hurting people everywhere—in our neighborhoods, our workplaces, and even in our own families and churches. Compassion is always in demand, and let's strive to fill that demand in every way we can.

1 Corinthians 10:1–13
Pride Will Take You Down

Now I want you to know, brothers, that our fathers were all under the cloud, all passed through the sea, and all were baptized into Moses in the cloud and in the sea. They all ate the same spiritual food, and all drank the same spiritual drink. For they drank from a spiritual rock that followed them, and that rock was Christ. But God was not pleased with most of them, for they were struck down in the wilderness.

Now these things became examples for us, so that we will not desire evil things as they did. Don't become idolaters as some of them were; as it is written, The people sat down to eat and drink, and got up to play. Let us not commit sexual immorality as some of them did, and in a single day 23,000 people fell dead. Let us not test Christ as some of them did and were destroyed by snakes. Nor should we complain as some of them did, and were killed by the destroyer. Now these things happened to them as examples, and they were written as a warning to us, on whom the ends of the ages have come. So, whoever thinks he stands must be careful not to fall. No temptation has overtaken you except what is common to humanity. God is faithful, and He will not allow you to be tempted beyond what you are able, but with the temptation

*He will also provide a way of escape so that you
are able to bear it.*

The testimony of an eyewitness is important in a court of law. Why? He or she was present and actually saw what happened.

God chose Moses to lead the nation of Israel out of Egyptian bondage. As they traveled toward the land God promised, they witnessed firsthand God's provision and protection. In a miraculous way God gave them food from heaven to eat and water from a rock. His cloud of protection surrounded them. But soon they forgot and behaved in a manner that displeased God. As a result, many perished in the wilderness and never received the blessings God intended for them to have.

In today's passage, Paul cautions believers about the sin of unbelief and disobedience. He gives examples from the past as object lessons when one deliberately chooses to disobey God and follows his own fleshly instincts instead of trusting in the Lord.

It's easy to look at the Israelites and shake our heads at their lack of faith after the miracles they had seen with their own eyes. "I just can't believe they could *walk through the Red Sea* and then not trust God!" we say. "How could they forget what God had done? I would never do such a thing!" But all too often, we too forget lessons we should have learned from the past. Is your lifestyle one that exemplifies a life of trust and obedience to a faithful God?

Acts 20:17–27
Sincere Devotion

Now from Miletus, he sent to Ephesus and called for the elders of the church. And when they came to him, he said to them: "You know, from the first day I set foot in Asia, how I was with you the whole time—serving the Lord with all humility, with tears, and with the trials that came to me through the plots of the Jews—and that I did not shrink back from proclaiming to you anything that was profitable or from teaching it to you in public and from house to house. I testified to both Jews and Greeks about repentance toward God and faith in our Lord Jesus.

"And now I am on my way to Jerusalem, bound in my spirit, not knowing what I will encounter there, except that in town after town the Holy Spirit testifies to me that chains and afflictions are waiting for me. But I count my life of no value to myself, so that I may finish my course and the ministry I received from the Lord Jesus, to testify to the gospel of God's grace.

"And now I know that none of you will ever see my face again—everyone I went about preaching the kingdom to. Therefore I testify to you this day that I am innocent of everyone's blood, for I did not shrink back from declaring to you the whole plan of God."

Saul, the well-known Pharisee and persecutor of Christians, was radically transformed into the apostle Paul—the self-denying, letter-writing missionary who met Jesus on the road to Damascus. Paul was chosen by God to be an instrument for taking the Good News to the Gentiles and to kings, as well as to the people of Israel (see Acts 9).

Paul was devoted to his calling even when faced with difficult circumstances and suffering. He endured hardships, knowing there was nothing more important than finishing the work the Lord had given him. Unlike many of us, he traveled from place to place, knowing that his time with those whom he preached to would be short. He would share the gospel, establish churches, and then move on to the next place God led him to. It couldn't have been easy to be constantly leaving those with whom he had shared the gospel and established a relationship.

In Christ, each of us has been given special tasks to do that play a part in spreading the gospel. Being sincerely devoted and unwavering in our calling is essential to being fruitful, in the midst of the circumstances God has placed us in. Whether we stay in one place or move from area to area like Paul did, our ultimate calling remains the same—to share the love of Jesus with those we encounter. Let's strive to be as devoted to this calling as Paul was.

James 5:13–18
Our Lifeline

*Is anyone among you suffering? He should
pray. Is anyone cheerful? He should sing praises.
Is anyone among you sick? He should call for the
elders of the church, and they should pray over him
after anointing him with olive oil in the name of the
Lord. The prayer of faith will save the sick person, and the Lord will restore him to health; if he
has committed sins, he will be forgiven. Therefore,
confess your sins to one another and pray for one
another, so that you may be healed. The urgent
request of a righteous person is very powerful in its
effect. Elijah was a man with a nature like ours; yet
he prayed earnestly that it would not rain, and for
three years and six months it did not rain on the
land. Then he prayed again, and the sky gave rain
and the land produced its fruit.*

It is amazing to think that God is willing to hear our prayers, our
cries for help, and our intercession for others. It seems implausible
that the God of creation, who sustains all life, would take note of the
pleas from our lives. But, because of His great love, He is happy to
answer our prayers.

James instructs believers to pray about everything. If you are
suffering or joyful, then pray. When people are sick, immediately lift

them before the Lord. Confess your sins to fellow believers, and pray for each other.

This all brings to mind Paul's exhortation in 1 Thessalonians 5:17: "Pray constantly." Did the apostle Paul mean we should be on our knees in prayer twenty-four hours a day, seven days a week? That seems unlikely. After all, Paul would later tell this same congregation, "If anyone isn't willing to work, he should not eat" (2 Thess. 3:10). How can we find time to work or eat if we spend all of our time in prayer?

In the original Greek language, the word translated as "constantly" denotes a recurrent action. In other words, Paul wasn't saying we should spend all day, every day, in prayer. He was saying that we should pray regularly and repeatedly.

Additionally, in the passage above, James ties together confession and intercession. Don't avoid one for the other. God desires to cleanse your heart when you confess your sins. He is also happy to hear you prioritize others above yourself. As the Lord sees your faith, He is pleased to answer your prayers.

This teaching from James comes with a beautiful promise. Your prayers have a powerful effect when offered from a righteous life. Today, you can make a powerful impact in the spiritual realm and in the world around you because of your prayers.

1 Peter 2:1–10
The Reason for Being

So rid yourselves of all malice, all deceit, hypocrisy, envy, and all slander. Like newborn infants, desire the pure spiritual milk, so that you may grow by it for your salvation, since you have tasted that the Lord is good. Coming to Him, a living stone— rejected by men but chosen and valuable to God— you yourselves, as living stones, are being built into a spiritual house for a holy priesthood to offer spiritual sacrifices acceptable to God through Jesus Christ. For it is contained in Scripture: "Look! I lay a stone in Zion, a chosen and honored cornerstone, and the one who believes in Him will never be put to shame!"

So honor will come to you who believe, but for the unbelieving, "The stone that the builders rejected—this One has become the cornerstone," and "A stone to stumble over, and a rock to trip over."

They stumble because they disobey the message; they were destined for this.

But you are a chosen race, a royal priesthood, a holy nation, a people for His possession, so that you may proclaim the praises of the One who called you out of darkness into His marvelous light. Once you were not a people, but now you are

*God's people; you had not received mercy, but now
you have received mercy.*

She had been adopted as an infant by an American family. Now, this newlywed Vietnamese woman sitting next to a gospel-sharing Christian on an airplane was fascinated by the idea that God, too, would adopt her into His family. She was in awe that the One who created the universe could love her and want her to be His child.

We hear the same awe in Peter's words: "Once you were not a people, but now you are God's people" (v. 10). In Christ, we have been made new! We are a chosen generation, a royal priesthood, a holy nation, a people of His own! Everyone has a desire to feel special, and Peter certainly gives us cause to celebrate here.

How can we not burst forth into singing? How can we not be filled with glory and praise? Our loving Heavenly Father, our "Abba," has delivered us from the kingdom of darkness where we were shackled. He has brought us into His marvelous light!

This text is not a command; it is an explanation. We breathe because we are alive. We praise because we are alive in Christ! Because of who He is in us, our being and our identity are in Him alone.

Take a few moments right now to "proclaim the praises of the One who called you out of darkness into His marvelous light"!

Romans 6:1–11
A Picture of New Life

What should we say then? Should we continue in sin so that grace may multiply? Absolutely not! How can we who died to sin still live in it? Or are you unaware that all of us who were baptized into Christ Jesus were baptized into His death? Therefore we were buried with Him by baptism into death, in order that, just as Christ was raised from the dead by the glory of the Father, so we too may walk in a new way of life. For if we have been joined with Him in the likeness of His death, we will certainly also be in the likeness of His resurrection. For we know that our old self was crucified with Him in order that sin's dominion over the body may be abolished, so that we may no longer be enslaved to sin, since a person who has died is freed from sin's claims. Now if we died with Christ, we believe that we will also live with Him, because we know that Christ, having been raised from the dead, will not die again. Death no longer rules over Him. For in light of the fact that He died, He died to sin once for all; but in light of the fact that He lives, He lives to God. So, you too consider yourselves dead to sin but alive to God in Christ Jesus.

Springtime provides a perfect picture of new life. The blooming flowers and trees all but erase the memory of cold winter days. The newness is special, refreshing, invigorating.

Without the lifelessness of winter, the newness of spring would be impossible. The dramatic contrast between the seasons heightens our awareness of the change. A similar change occurs in believers as they are born again into God's family by faith in Jesus Christ. This new birth cannot occur unless it is preceded by death, and Jesus paved the way for us by His own death on the cross.

When we follow Jesus in believers' baptism, we present the world a picture of new spiritual life. We proclaim the death of our old self and a new way of living. When new believers are baptized, pastors often speak of how going under the water symbolizes death, and raising back up represents new life. Many will use wording that paraphrases Romans 6:4: "Buried with Him in the likeness of His death, raised with Him in the likeness of His resurrection to walk in the newness of life."

When buds begin to emerge on the branches of a tree, we know that new leaves and new growth will follow. Likewise, our new life should be obvious to others as we walk in it. Is your life a testament to "a new way of life"?

Acts 24:10–21
Want a Clear Conscience?

When the governor motioned to him to speak, Paul replied: "Because I know you have been a judge of this nation for many years, I am glad to offer my defense in what concerns me. You are able to determine that it is no more than 12 days since I went up to worship in Jerusalem. They didn't find me disputing with anyone or causing a disturbance among the crowd, either in the temple complex or in the synagogues or anywhere in the city. Neither can they provide evidence to you of what they now bring against me. But I confess this to you: I worship my fathers' God according to the Way, which they call a sect, believing all the things that are written in the Law and in the Prophets. And I have a hope in God, which these men themselves also accept, that there is going to be a resurrection, both of the righteous and the unrighteous. I always do my best to have a clear conscience toward God and men. After many years, I came to bring charitable gifts and offerings to my nation, and while I was doing this, some Jews from Asia found me ritually purified in the temple, without a crowd and without any uproar. It is they who ought to be here before you to bring charges, if they have anything against me. Either let these men here state what wrongdoing they found in me

*when I stood before the Sanhedrin, or about this
one statement I cried out while standing among
them, 'Today I am being judged before you concerning the resurrection of the dead.'"*

A s we go about working in the mission of God, our character often
will be called into question. Our motives will be scrutinized, and
our actions will be judged. In the early church, Paul often defended
himself before the accusations of many people, including those who
were politically powerful and those who were the religious leaders of
the day.

We will likely not be called upon to answer for our faith in court,
but we must be able to give a witness for our faith in the culture. It
begins with living in such a way that God is pleased with our lives. Our
integrity before others is dependent upon our integrity before God. As
we daily submit to the work of Christ in our lives, then our character
is changed to mirror that of Jesus.

Paul described the experience of having a clear conscience so that
others would know he was certain of what he believed. Our actions will
always show off our true beliefs. If we want to have a conscience like
Paul, we must have similar convictions—and hold to them.

The only way to a clear conscience? Have a sure faith.

Ephesians 5:18–33
Submit to Each Other

Be filled by the Spirit: speaking to one another in psalms, hymns, and spiritual songs, singing and making music from your heart to the Lord, giving thanks always for everything to God the Father in the name of our Lord Jesus Christ, submitting to one another in the fear of Christ.

Wives, submit to your own husbands as to the Lord, for the husband is the head of the wife as Christ is the head of the church. He is the Savior of the body. Now as the church submits to Christ, so wives are to submit to their husbands in everything. Husbands, love your wives, just as Christ loved the church and gave Himself for her to make her holy, cleansing her with the washing of water by the word. He did this to present the church to Himself in splendor, without spot or wrinkle or anything like that, but holy and blameless. In the same way, husbands are to love their wives as their own bodies. He who loves his wife loves himself. For no one ever hates his own flesh but provides and cares for it, just as Christ does for the church, since we are members of His body.

For this reason a man will leave his father and mother and be joined to his wife, and the two will become one flesh.

This mystery is profound, but I am talking about
Christ and the church. To sum up, each one of
you is to love his wife as himself, and the wife is to
respect her husband.

When we see the red octagon with the letters S-T-O-P, we know what we are supposed to do. The same goes for the red traffic light; we stop. We merge when a lane is closed. We slow down in a school zone. We submit to the signs. We acknowledge the legitimacy of the rules of the road and the power of our government.

We give honor and obedience to civil authority because it has been set up by God for the good of man. Most of us are not doing it blindly, because we know the consequences of receiving a ticket or, worse yet, causing an accident.

So why do we struggle when Paul tells the Ephesians to submit to one another? Women might bristle sometimes that wives should submit to their husbands, because he is the head of the wife. But at the same time, husbands are commanded to love their wives just as Christ loved the church. And yes, the church certainly must submit to Christ, who gave Himself for all of us.

All of this submission business is to be conducted under the fear of God. We know that fear involves reverence, and we revere God out of the respect that is deep admiration, based on who He is and what He has done. And out of this reverence and respect, we should obey and submit to His commands.

1 Peter 3:1–12
Reflect Christ

In the same way, wives, submit yourselves to your own husbands so that, even if some disobey the Christian message, they may be won over without a message by the way their wives live when they observe your pure, reverent lives. Your beauty should not consist of outward things like elaborate hairstyles and the wearing of gold ornaments or fine clothes. Instead, it should consist of what is inside the heart with the imperishable quality of a gentle and quiet spirit, which is very valuable in God's eyes. For in the past, the holy women who put their hope in God also beautified themselves in this way, submitting to their own husbands, just as Sarah obeyed Abraham, calling him lord. You have become her children when you do what is good and are not frightened by anything alarming.

Husbands, in the same way, live with your wives with an understanding of their weaker nature yet showing them honor as coheirs of the grace of life, so that your prayers will not be hindered.

Now finally, all of you should be like-minded and sympathetic, should love believers, and be compassionate and humble, not paying back evil for evil or insult for insult but, on the contrary, giving a blessing, since you were called for this, so that you can inherit a blessing.

For the one who wants to love life and to see good days must keep his tongue from evil and his lips from speaking deceit, and he must turn away from evil and do what is good. He must seek peace and pursue it, because the eyes of the Lord are on the righteous and His ears are open to their request. But the face of the Lord is against those who do what is evil.

In a family, each person has his or her role(s) to play. Perhaps you're a grandmother, a mother, or a sister. Maybe you're a grandfather, a husband, or a nephew. In the first part of chapter 3, Peter spoke specifically to the roles that a wife and a husband play in a marriage. There are character traits unique to the man and unique to the woman. But beginning in verse 8, Peter shared those qualities that everyone as Christians must possess.

These characteristics reflect the person of Jesus Christ. Just as He was (and is) sympathetic, loving, compassionate, and humble, we are to be the same. Just as He blessed those who did evil against Him (even to the point of praying for those who sent Him to the cross), we are to do the same.

We must strive to be more like Christ in our homes, in our workplaces, and in our communities. There's no greater witness we can have for the gospel than our character and the manner in which we live our lives.

Matthew 20:20-28
How to Spend Your Life

Then the mother of Zebedee's sons approached Him with her sons. She knelt down to ask Him for something. "What do you want?" He asked her.

"Promise," she said to Him, "that these two sons of mine may sit, one on Your right and the other on Your left, in Your kingdom."

But Jesus answered, "You don't know what you're asking. Are you able to drink the cup that I am about to drink?"

"We are able," they said to Him.

He told them, "You will indeed drink My cup. But to sit at My right and left is not Mine to give; instead, it belongs to those for whom it has been prepared by My Father." When the 10 disciples heard this, they became indignant with the two brothers. But Jesus called them over and said, "You know that the rulers of the Gentiles dominate them, and the men of high position exercise power over them. It must not be like that among you. On the contrary, whoever wants to become great among you must be your servant, and whoever wants to be first among you must be your slave; just as the Son of Man did not come to be served, but to serve, and to give His life—a ransom for many."

Ho ow would you answer if someone asked you, "How should I spend my life?" Jesus answered that question by telling His disciples to spend their lives living and dying for others. He is the supreme model for that teaching.

America's second highest military honor is The Distinguished Service Cross. Criteria include risk of life and merit above all other medals except one. The nation's highest award is The Medal of Honor. The one who gets this medal is often deceased, because he gave his life to get it. But they didn't die so they would get the award; they died in order to save the lives of others. These awards recognize what Jesus taught about greatness—giving your life for others is the ultimate honor.

Jesus told us that the way to greatness is service. He taught that the greatest will die to save others. They won't oppress others and demand those people do the hard, dirty, risky work. Instead, the greatest will do that work themselves. They will sacrifice their own comfort and perhaps their own lives in service to others.

As Jesus moved toward the cross, two disciples wanted greatness. The other disciples were angry with envy. Jesus defused the disciples' pursuit of position by testifying that He hadn't come to be a slave-master but a slave—who would give His life to save all other lives.

Most of us aren't in a position where we need to or can physically give our lives for others. But we are all capable of giving up the things that make us comfortable if that is what it takes to help save others' spiritual lives.

That's the answer of how to spend your life! It's the way to greatness.

1 Peter 4:12–19
The Blessing of Suffering

Dear friends, don't be surprised when the fiery ordeal comes among you to test you as if some-thing unusual were happening to you. Instead, rejoice as you share in the sufferings of the Messiah, so that you may also rejoice with great joy at the revelation of His glory. If you are ridiculed for the name of Christ, you are blessed, because the Spirit of glory and of God rests on you. None of you, however, should suffer as a murderer, a thief, an evildoer, or a meddler. But if anyone suffers as a "Christian," he should not be ashamed but should glorify God in having that name. For the time has come for judgment to begin with God's household, and if it begins with us, what will the outcome be for those who disobey the gospel of God?

And if a righteous person is saved with dif-ficulty, what will become of the ungodly and the sinner?

So those who suffer according to God's will should, while doing what is good, entrust them-selves to a faithful Creator.

Dietrich Bonhoeffer was a German pastor who resisted Hitler in Nazi Germany. At a time when much of the church in Germany was turning a blind eye to the evil around them in order to escape persecution, Bonhoeffer could not. He believed that the true church must suffer in a godless world. In his classic book *The Cost of Discipleship*, Bonhoeffer, who was hanged by the Nazis just weeks before the end of World War II, said, "The worse the evil, the readier must the Christian be to suffer; he must let the evil person fall into Jesus' hands."

Even though the Nazis hanged Bonhoeffer, his suffering is still glorifying God today. He loved the authors of his suffering because he wanted them to see the love of Christ. He knew that suffering was the price of overcoming evil with love. In fact, the camp doctor who witnessed the execution of Bonhoeffer never forgot the picture of humble obedience and love portrayed by the man going to his death. It changed that doctor.

Would someone witnessing your suffering see enough of the love of Jesus in you to change them? Does the way you deal with your spouse's diagnosis of a degenerative disease show the world that you trust God or that you have no hope for the future? Does your response to a great financial loss reveal your belief that God will provide for all your needs, or does it reveal a lack of trust in Him?

There are so many ways we can show our faith to the world, and none may be more powerful than the way we react to suffering. Let this be our prayer: "Father, when I suffer, let me glorify You so that others see Your love."

Quote: Dietrich Bonhoeffer, *The Cost of Discipleship* (New York: Touchstone, 1959), 142.

Acts 10:34–45
All Are Welcome

Then Peter began to speak: "Now I really under-
stand that God doesn't show favoritism, but in
every nation the person who fears Him and does
righteousness is acceptable to Him. He sent the
message to the Israelites, proclaiming the good
news of peace through Jesus Christ—He is Lord of
all. You know the events that took place throughout
Judea, beginning from Galilee after the baptism
that John preached: how God anointed Jesus of
Nazareth with the Holy Spirit and with power, and
how He went about doing good and healing all
who were under the tyranny of the Devil, because
God was with Him. We ourselves are witnesses of
everything He did in both the Judean country and
in Jerusalem, yet they killed Him by hanging Him
on a tree. God raised up this man on the third
day and permitted Him to be seen, not by all the
people, but by us, witnesses appointed beforehand
by God, who ate and drank with Him after He rose
from the dead. He commanded us to preach to
the people and to solemnly testify that He is the
One appointed by God to be the Judge of the
living and the dead. All the prophets testify about
Him that through His name everyone who believes
in Him will receive forgiveness of sins."

While Peter was still speaking these words, the Holy Spirit came down on all those who heard the message. The circumcised believers who had come with Peter were astounded because the gift of the Holy Spirit had been poured out on the Gentiles also.

Historically it was against religious protocol for Jews to associate with Gentiles. In the previous verses of Acts 10, the Holy Spirit revealed to Peter that no person, regardless of race or ethnicity, should be considered common or unclean. He was then sent to the home of Cornelius, a Gentile, to tell him about Jesus Christ, His death on the cross, and His resurrection from the dead. Cornelius and his entire household heard the message, believed, and received the Holy Spirit.

Then and now, the gospel is for every person on Earth. Jesus' arms were spread wide on the cross to welcome people from every tribe, tongue, and nation into His kingdom. God's missionary heart beats for all people to know and worship Him. We are called by God to join Him in His mission to grow His church and carry the gospel into the entire world.

For many of us, sharing the gospel with the nations doesn't even require a passport. God is bringing the nations to our neighborhoods.

Who is God telling you to welcome? The Muslim refugee family on the third floor who are having a difficult transition partly because many of your neighbors are worried they may be terrorists? The Indian couple down the street who have a trove of gods prominently displayed in their home? The checkout girl at the convenience store who wears only black and has an inverted pentagram tattooed on her neck? All need to hear the good news of Jesus, and all are welcome.

Ephesians 6:10–18
Top-Quality Protective Gear

Finally, be strengthened by the Lord and by His vast strength. Put on the full armor of God so that you can stand against the tactics of the Devil. For our battle is not against flesh and blood, but against the rulers, against the authorities, against the world powers of this darkness, against the spiritual forces of evil in the heavens. This is why you must take up the full armor of God, so that you may be able to resist in the evil day, and having prepared everything, to take your stand.

Stand, therefore, with truth like a belt around your waist, righteousness like armor on your chest, and your feet sandaled with readiness for the gospel of peace. In every situation take the shield of faith, and with it you will be able to extinguish all the flaming arrows of the evil one. Take the helmet of salvation, and the sword of the Spirit, which is God's word.

Pray at all times in the Spirit with every prayer and request, and stay alert in this with all perseverance and intercession for all the saints.

Have you ever seen a S.W.A.T. team's tactical gear? Those men and women are well covered by armor and equipped with the weapons and training that will help them resist even the most well-armed enemy.

In a lesser way, protective equipment is often used by first-responders such as police officers and firefighters. Football players are required to wear protective gear to prevent injuries. Even children are required to put on bike helmets for short rides just in case of accidents. One thing is for certain, without protective gear, people would be needlessly injured and others would not be able to do their jobs safely.

Ephesians 6 tells us that we are in a spiritual fight with unseen forces. Just because we don't see them doesn't make them less real, less dangerous, or less worthy of our being equipped to resist them. We need some top-quality protective gear! Thankfully, the Lord has provided all we need.

The apostle Paul listed our gear: the helmet of salvation, the shield of faith, the sword of the Spirit, the breastplate of righteousness, and our feet shod with the gospel of peace. And don't forget that we have the Truth.

It would be nice if God had simply said He would keep Satan away from us, but that is not the case. The enemy will attack us, but with God's protection and the knowledge that ultimately God has already won the battle against him, we can stand, and stand strong.

It is important to note that all of the gear mentioned is worn on the front of the body, and a sword can only be used well when we are facing our enemy. Retreat is not an option in this battle; we would surely lose. Instead, let us face the Devil with all of the resources God has given us.

2 Peter 3:1–9
Mercy in God's Delays

Dear friends, this is now the second letter I have written to you; in both letters, I want to develop a genuine understanding with a reminder, so that you can remember the words previously spoken by the holy prophets and the command of our Lord and Savior given through your apostles. First, be aware of this: Scoffers will come in the last days to scoff, living according to their own desires, saying, "Where is the promise of His coming? Ever since the fathers fell asleep, all things continue as they have been since the beginning of creation." They willfully ignore this: Long ago the heavens and the earth were brought about from water and through water by the word of God. Through these waters the world of that time perished when it was flooded. But by the same word, the present heavens and earth are stored up for fire, being kept until the day of judgment and destruction of ungodly men.

Dear friends, don't let this one thing escape you: With the Lord one day is like a thousand years, and a thousand years like one day. The Lord does not delay His promise, as some understand delay, but is patient with you, not wanting any to perish but all to come to repentance.

Every few years, a local news station runs a series on the imminent danger of living near a major earthquake fault line. Twenty-five years ago, on five successive nights, newscasters breathlessly warned viewers to expect the "Big One" within the next fifty years. They suggested ways to earthquake-proof your house and urged everyone to keep a supply of fresh water and canned food on hand. Recently, the same news station aired another five-night series of breathless warnings: expect the "Big One" within the next fifty years!

The problem is that the more the media talks about something that they predict will happen, but it *doesn't* happen, the less people listen to them. The audience just tunes out and goes on with their lives. It's similar to when a parent constantly threatens a child with punishment but never follows through. At first, the child might be concerned, but when he learns there's nothing behind the words, he pays no attention to the parent's threats.

It is easy to grow complacent when news of anticipated doom doesn't happen! The apostle Peter knew it would be like that for God's people. Nearing the end of his life, he reminded the scattered churches to be mindful of the Lord's imminent return and the need for all to come to repentance.

Why hasn't He come yet? We don't know. But His tarrying will give us time to tell one more family member, friend, or neighbor of God's redeeming grace and love through Jesus Christ.

1 John 3:10–18
Love Is a Verb

*Whoever does not do what is right is not of God,
especially the one who does not love his brother.
For this is the message you have heard from the
beginning: We should love one another, unlike Cain,
who was of the evil one and murdered his brother.
And why did he murder him? Because his works
were evil, and his brother's were righteous. Do
not be surprised, brothers, if the world hates you.
We know that we have passed from death to life
because we love our brothers. The one who does
not love remains in death. Everyone who hates his
brother is a murderer, and you know that no murderer has eternal life residing in him.*

*This is how we have come to know love: He
laid down His life for us. We should also lay down
our lives for our brothers. If anyone has this world's
goods and sees his brother in need but closes his
eyes to his need—how can God's love reside in him?*

*Little children, we must not love with word or
speech, but with truth and action.*

I n the 1990s, a popular Christian band sang a song titled "Love Is a
Verb." The song stood out for several reasons. First, how many song
titles have the word *verb* in them? And second, and more importantly,
the majority of the countless songs that have been written about love

have described it as an emotion. And we all know that emotions come and go. They are fickle, and we cannot count on them to sustain something as important as love.

The Bible clearly describes love as a verb—an action. In this first letter penned by the aging, beloved apostle John, he reminds his readers that the evidence of a genuine conversion is our love toward others. Because Christ died for us, we should also be willing to give our lives for others. The love of Christ that drew us to Him is our motivation to love one another. Showing love for others shows that we are true followers of Christ.

In verse 12, John pointed to Cain—"who was of the evil one"—as a negative example. Cain was the antithesis of godly love. Cain's murder of his brother, Abel, proved Cain to be a child of wickedness. His actions showed that he did not love his brother. Our actions need to show that we *do* love others.

The gospel transforms; it is the ultimate change agent! And Christ is our example of love. John 3:16 and Romans 5:8 remind us that He is the highest demonstration of God's love for humanity. By His death on the cross, He demonstrated the fullness of sacrificial love. Through the power of His Spirit dwelling within us, we can love others as He loves us.

Galatians 5:16–25
Spirit Versus Flesh

I say then, walk by the Spirit and you will not carry out the desire of the flesh. For the flesh desires what is against the Spirit, and the Spirit desires what is against the flesh; these are opposed to each other, so that you don't do what you want. But if you are led by the Spirit, you are not under the law.

Now the works of the flesh are obvious: sexual immorality, moral impurity, promiscuity, idolatry, sorcery, hatreds, strife, jealousy, outbursts of anger, selfish ambitions, dissensions, factions, envy, drunkenness, carousing, and anything similar. I tell you about these things in advance—as I told you before—that those who practice such things will not inherit the kingdom of God.

But the fruit of the Spirit is love, joy, peace, patience, kindness, goodness, faith, gentleness, self-control. Against such things there is no law. Now those who belong to Christ Jesus have crucified the flesh with its passions and desires. Since we live by the Spirit, we must also follow the Spirit.

Children of all ages like to play tug-of-war (and adults have been known to really get into it as well!). As they team up on either end of a long rope, they combine their strength so they can pull the opposing team across the center line. The struggle shows itself in the tension placed on the rope. If the teams are evenly matched, the game can take awhile. But if one team is stronger than the other, it can be over in the blink of an eye.

A tough competition like tug-of-war provides a great image of the stress we may face as we seek to serve the Lord. Our struggles in discipleship are revealed in the tension pulling us in two directions at the same time. The tug-of-war puts a strain on our walk with Him.

Paul wrote about the tension in terms of the Spirit and the flesh. Because we belong to Christ, our desire should be to follow the leadership of the Holy Spirit in a selfless way. However, we have to resist the temptation to feed the sinful, selfish indulgences—"the works of the flesh"—that do not honor the Lord. When we read Paul's list above, we see that we are all guilty of giving in to the works of the flesh. It is so easy to fall into them if we are not careful.

Paul teaches us that winning the battle every day starts by walking in the Spirit. Each day finds us prayerfully resolving that we are going to follow and obey Jesus step by step. When we walk in the Spirit, our internal game of tug-of-war will have a quick and clear winner every time. And when the Spirit wins, we—and others—will see the resulting fruit of love, joy, peace, patience, kindness, goodness, faith, gentleness, and self-control.

1 John 4:1–6
Truth Versus Error

Dear friends, do not believe every spirit, but test the spirits to determine if they are from God, because many false prophets have gone out into the world.

This is how you know the Spirit of God: Every spirit who confesses that Jesus Christ has come in the flesh is from God. But every spirit who does not confess Jesus is not from God. This is the spirit of the antichrist; you have heard that he is coming, and he is already in the world now.

You are from God, little children, and you have conquered them, because the One who is in you is greater than the one who is in the world. They are from the world. Therefore what they say is from the world, and the world listens to them. We are from God. Anyone who knows God listens to us; anyone who is not from God does not listen to us. From this we know the Spirit of truth and the spirit of deception.

H ave you ever been in a conversation with someone who offered "godly" advice or insight, and something in your heart tightened up? It just did not seem to align with what you have been taught. If you know for certain the information is false, you can correct the error on the spot. If you do not, the moment can become awkward and uncomfortable. You smile and nod your head, waiting for the time to end so you can check the facts for yourself.

Or perhaps you hear a pastor speaking on the radio or on TV, and he's talking about a topic such as what Jesus had to say about humility. Sounds like a great thing to talk about. What he says seems good and right to you, and you note that this guy is a *great* communicator. But then he talks about how Jesus was a great teacher, but there were other great teachers, too, like Muhammad, Confucius, and the Dalai Lama. We need to take their teachings into consideration too, alongside Jesus' teachings. Wait. You know *that's* not right. You don't even need to check your Bible for that one.

John wrote this first letter of three to warn believers of the false prophets seeping into their churches, teaching what probably sounded a lot like "Jesus talk." John told them, "[you] are from God. Anyone who knows God listens to us" (v. 6).

We do not ever have to grab onto the first thing we hear and believe it is true. When there is doubt, take the time to read God's Word. Ask others you trust for godly wisdom. Seek God's face in prayer. As a loving heavenly Father, He will always answer.

1 Thessalonians 5:1–8
The Lord's Return

*About the times and the seasons: Brothers,
you do not need anything to be written to you.
For you yourselves know very well that the Day
of the Lord will come just like a thief in the night.
When they say, "Peace and security," then sudden
destruction comes on them, like labor pains come
on a pregnant woman, and they will not escape.
But you, brothers, are not in the dark, for this day
to overtake you like a thief. For you are all sons of
light and sons of the day. We do not belong to the
night or the darkness. So then, we must not sleep,
like the rest, but we must stay awake and be serious. For those who sleep, sleep at night, and those
who get drunk are drunk at night. But since we
belong to the day, we must be serious and put the
armor of faith and love on our chests, and put on
a helmet of the hope of salvation.*

Every year it seems as though someone proclaims it is *the* year that the Lord will return. Books are written about it; there are even billboards giving an exact date as to Christ's return. There are so-called end-times experts that claim to know the date of Jesus' return and proclaim it to whoever will listen, and then when it doesn't happen, they just change the date.

Some will point to signs such as natural disasters, wars, famine, and the like to predict that Jesus is coming back soon. After all, in Matthew 24:7, Jesus told His disciples those things would herald His coming. But those kinds of things have happened throughout history. There doesn't seem to be anything special about the ones we are having now that are any worse than those in the past. In fact, many would claim that the world is in a better state now than at many times in the past two millennia.

The fact of the matter is there is really no way to know exactly when Christ will return.

In 1 Thessalonians, Paul writes about Christ's return. He lets his readers know it will come suddenly and unexpectedly, just like a thief might overtake you. Yet this is not a cause of concern for Paul. How can believers feel comforted, knowing Christ will come again, yet they will have no knowledge of when it will happen?

But as believers we know all we need to know concerning the day of the Lord's return. The only information we need to know is a person: Jesus Himself. If we are believers who know Christ, we are prepared for His return, so day or date does not matter. In God's time, Jesus will return. Until then, let's spend the time we have introducing more people to Him.

Thank the Lord right now for His salvation. Thank Him that we do not need to walk in anxiety regarding Jesus' return but can await it expectantly.

Revelation 1:1–8
He Was, He Is, and He Will Be

The revelation of Jesus Christ that God gave Him to show His slaves what must quickly take place. He sent it and signified it through His angel to His slave John, who testified to God's word and to the testimony about Jesus Christ, in all he saw. The one who reads this is blessed, and those who hear the words of this prophecy and keep what is written in it are blessed, because the time is near!

John:

To the seven churches in Asia.

Grace and peace to you from the One who is, who was, and who is coming; from the seven spirits before His throne; and from Jesus Christ, the faithful witness, the firstborn from the dead and the ruler of the kings of the earth.

To Him who loves us and has set us free from our sins by His blood, and made us a kingdom, priests to His God and Father—the glory and dominion are His forever and ever. Amen.

Look! He is coming with the clouds, and every eye will see Him, including those who pierced Him. And all the families of the earth will mourn over Him. This is certain. Amen.

"I am the Alpha and the Omega," says the Lord God, "the One who is, who was, and who is coming, the Almighty."

Many of us want to know the end when we're at the beginning—we look at the last chapter of the book just to see if it ends well. During a season of tribulation and isolation, Jesus essentially said to John, "Remember, I was already there at creation and will continue forever. I am here with you." We can trust that, too.

Jesus assures us that He has the final word: He is the Alpha and the Omega; the first Word and the Last; our hope and security in the future, as well as in the present.

There are many things that can strike fear in our hearts—disease, terrorism, natural disasters, loss of a loved one. But we know that Jesus is with us in the midst of those tragedies, and we know He always will be. We know this because He told us so.

Revelation reminds us that God's plan has a determined end. When things around us falter, remember He is there; nothing catches God off-guard. He calls us to trust Him. He is our rock and safe refuge at all times. Today's passage assures us that He is in control, and He knows the end—even from the beginning!

Thank God right now for the security of knowing that He was, is, and always will be in control. Trust Him for all your needs today and those yet to come.

2 Timothy 4:1–8
Endurance

I solemnly charge you before God and Christ Jesus, who is going to judge the living and the dead, and because of His appearing and His kingdom: Proclaim the message; persist in it whether convenient or not; rebuke, correct, and encourage with great patience and teaching. For the time will come when they will not tolerate sound doctrine, but according to their own desires, will multiply teachers for themselves because they have an itch to hear something new. They will turn away from hearing the truth and will turn aside to myths. But as for you, be serious about everything, endure hardship, do the work of an evangelist, fulfill your ministry.

For I am already being poured out as a drink offering, and the time for my departure is close. I have fought the good fight, I have finished the race, I have kept the faith. There is reserved for me in the future the crown of righteousness, which the Lord, the righteous Judge, will give me on that day, and not only to me, but to all those who have loved His appearing.

P aul's second letter to Timothy was an encouraging reminder of Timothy's spiritual heritage and personal faith. But Paul also warned Timothy of perilous times and perilous people who would creep into the church, having a form of godliness, but denying the power of God. Paul concludes this warning with a charge: Preach the Word! To those who don't want to hear sound doctrine, whose ears itch to hear only what pleases them, who turn from truth to worldly philosophy: Preach the Word! This charge, along with its subsequent challenge to endure afflictions, is especially relevant to anyone who carries a role in church leadership.

When the Word is preached or taught in its entirety, a believer runs the risk of being labeled legalistic, intolerant, or even out of touch with reality. Preaching the Word may offend. Church attendance could be impacted, and offerings might temporarily decline. But the charge in God's Word is clear: Teach the Word and endure the subsequent hardship. Spread the gospel and fulfill your ministry for the cause of Christ. Never forget what Christ endured for you.

Paul also reminded Timothy that finishing well is important. Though not without challenges and setbacks, Paul's Christian life had been a success due to his faithful and rugged devotion. Now, nearing the end of his life, Paul realized the full impact of his legacy was finally assured. He had invested his energies in the noble work of God's kingdom and remained faithful. Like Paul, despite our circumstances, we can endure to the end through loving devotion to God.

Revelation 21:21—22:5
No More Light

The 12 gates are 12 pearls; each individual gate was made of a single pearl. The broad street of the city was pure gold, like transparent glass.

I did not see a sanctuary in it, because the Lord God the Almighty and the Lamb are its sanctuary. The city does not need the sun or the moon to shine on it, because God's glory illuminates it, and its lamp is the Lamb. The nations will walk in its light, and the kings of the earth will bring their glory into it. Each day its gates will never close because it will never be night there. They will bring the glory and honor of the nations into it. Nothing profane will ever enter it: no one who does what is vile or false, but only those written in the Lamb's book of life.

Then he showed me the river of living water, sparkling like crystal, flowing from the throne of God and of the Lamb down the middle of the broad street of the city. The tree of life was on both sides of the river, bearing 12 kinds of fruit, producing its fruit every month. The leaves of the tree are for healing the nations, and there will no longer be any curse. The throne of God and of the Lamb will be in the city, and His slaves will serve Him. They will see His face, and His name will be on their foreheads. Night will no longer exist, and people will not need lamplight or sunlight, because the Lord God will give them light. And they will reign forever and ever.

God's plan from the beginning of creation has been to bring a world of worshippers to Himself. After Adam and Eve sinned, darkness entered the world, but God's plan never changed. He began the process of pushing back the darkness with His plan of redemption through Jesus, the Light of the world.

A room can be pitch black, yet with a flick of a switch, the darkness disappears and the room is illuminated. One little light bulb in a lamp can brighten an entire room, and how amazing is it that Jesus will illumine all of heaven?

In the book of Revelation, John gives us a glimpse into heaven. When describing the New Jerusalem, adorned with its beautiful jewels, pearly gates, and streets of pure gold, John reveals that Jesus is the light or lamp of God's glory. God's glory in this heavenly city is so radiant that it eliminates the need even for a sun or moon.

Practically speaking, a lamp holds a light. Through this imagery, John reveals that Jesus, the Lamb who was slain, contains the light of God's glory. In other words, God's glory is found in the Person of Christ. Therefore, the clearest place to see God's glory is to look at Jesus.

The good news is the story of His glory. His death, burial, and resurrection point us to that eternal glory that we will share with Him in heaven.